You Better Recognize!

A spiritual guide – because life's a "trip"

A guide to recognizing the light,
the joy and the power within.

"You Better Recognize" *phrase.* 1. An African-American
colloquialism. 2. Black slang.

Usage:
a) "You better give me the respect I'm due."
b) "You better pay attention to me."
c) "You better acknowledge my presence."

Summary: A spiritual guide because life's a "trip!"

Printed in the United States of America.

Roses Are READ Productions
P. O. Box 7844
St. Paul, MN 55107
E-mail: valerie.rose @gte.net
Websites:
http://www.rosesareread.cc
http://www.valerierose.com

Love Unlimited is the inspirational imprint of Roses Are READ, an organization which produces and publishes books in all genres.

ISBN: 0-9703489-1-6

Library of Congress Catalog Card Number: 2002096638.

Cover design: Associates By Design   http://www.designabd.com
Back Cover Photo: Tjoshua Ivory
Valerie's Makeup: Rhonda Jackson
Roses Are READ logo by Adrian Crawford

Foreword

You better recognize! Recognize what? Everything. Recognize one cannot be content with a lot, unless one can be content with a little. Our lives are often so fast paced that we too frequently fail to enjoy the small beauties encountered in everyday life. For far too many of us, that anticipated, glorious, promised "tomorrow" never comes as dreams remain deferred, postponed, and unrealized.

We must ask ourselves, "Do we really know what we want?" For example, there was a young man, we will call him Lee, who loved pancakes. In fact, Lee was a glutton for pancakes. His mother decided to cure her son of this problem. One Saturday morning, she got up and made Lee as many pancakes as he could eat. One after another he ate them as fast as she could make them. After about twenty small pancakes, Lee's mother asked, "Lee, do you want some more?" Lee replied, "No ma'am, I don't even want the ones I already ate." The irony is that even when Lee got what he wanted, he didn't want what he got. What really constitutes fulfillment? What really constitutes happiness? What really constitutes joy? What really constitutes success?

We must learn that our souls are not permanently satisfied by material possessions, but from an inner peace within our very souls. This inner peace transcends the ploys of marketing specialists, it transcends the "American Dream," it even transcends fraudulent religion. Inner peace is realized when we slow our world down; and, as we begin to slow down our world, we begin to recognize what is important in life and what is necessary for our soul to flourish.

You Better Recognize! A spiritual guide- because life's a "trip" provides readers with ideas on how to build positive self-concepts, self-discipline, self-efficacy, self-initiative, and self-preservation through truisms, heartwarming personal stories, poems and quotes. Valerie Rose expresses many poignant statements that all succinctly tie into the overarching thesis of her book. The thesis of her book is based on the universal *Law of Reciprocity* or *Sowing and Reaping*. Valerie Rose eloquently articulates to the reader potential the potential rewards and consequences of our actions. The beauty of this book is that it focuses on the self, the only aspect that we can control.

In Gary Zukav's *The Seat of the Soul*, he asks, "Who among us is an expert on the human experience?" In this rhetorical question he is unequivocally telling us no one is an expert on the human experience. However, he does believe that we can share our perceptions and prayerfully help others along their journey. Valerie Rose does not claim to be a "self-help guru," she does not give a 10 point to do list nor does she promise unattainable results. Valerie Rose simply pours her life learning experiences into a soulful literary piece in attempt to help lift others as she continues to climb toward "the light."

Life is a trip! Valerie Rose's work is carefully crafted around the many issues which make this life so seemingly complicated such as: finances, life goals, relationships and sex. Valerie Rose does not ignore or pretend that life does not present us with potential problems. Yet, in the same vein she reminds us of the words of John F. Kennedy, "When written in Chinese, the word crisis is composed of two characters. One represents danger, and the other represents opportunity." She emphatically convinces us to become the masters of our fates, the captains of our souls by recognizing that in the middle of crises comes opportunity for growth and knowledge.

Valerie is the epitome of her name, which means *power*, or *to be strong*; while still following suit with her second name, Rose, which is synonymous with beauty and love. Valerie Rose possesses combinations rarely found in today's society. She has beauty and intelligence. She is athletic and strong, yet incredibly feminine. She is a domestic and a career woman. Valerie Rose's literally skills are just as diverse and dynamic as her names. For example she can awaken your conscious to serious spiritual matters or burn your loins with steamy scenes from her debut novel, *Cappuccino in the Winter*.

Valerie Rose encourages those around her to live for today, while still considering tomorrow. She does not send one out on a self-indulgent fantasy, but inspires them to recognize the potential in themselves and every situation they encounter. Valerie Rose is not selling theoretical dreams, but actual life proven experiences- hers! She may not, yet, be a media darling, but she is a superstar in her own right.

Valerie Rose is an inspiration. Seven years ago I explained to Valerie that I wanted to go back to school for my Doctorate. When everyone else discouraged me from achieving this goal, Valerie encouraged me to reach for my dreams. I am now a Doctoral Candidate at an accredited university. Four years ago, I explained to Valerie how I dreamed of becoming a writer. When everyone one else snickered, Valerie encouraged me to reach my goals. Since that time I have co-written several book chapters and journal articles in my field of study (Educational Psychology). Two years ago, I told Valerie of my goal to begin a revolution of love in our world. When everyone else told me I was a radical visionary, Valerie told me to reach for my dreams. At this time, this goal is not accomplished, but **I WILL** initiate a movement, a revolution of love and peace along the lines of Jesus of Nazareth, Siddhartha Guatama (Buddha), Mohandas Gandhi, and Dr. Martin Luther King, Jr.. Thanks for not squashing my dreams, Aunt Val.

Doctoral Candidate Ramel L. Smith

Table of Contents

Recognition

There are many paths to God.
In my gratitude, I would like to *recognize* all of them:

God
The Creator
Universal Love
Nature
The Divine Infinite Spirit
The Force
The Almighty
The Universe
The Cosmos
Jesus
The Architect of the Universe
Universal Energy
The Master of the Universe
Invisible Force of Energy
The Supreme Being
Incomprehensible Love
Infinite Energy
One Love
The Great Spirit
The Light
Allah
Buddha
Jehovah
The Source
The Highest Form of Universal Intelligence
Love
All There Is

Peace and Joy Until You Reach the Light!

Acknowledgements

Thank you to the Divine Infinite Spirit – for my life.
Thank you, Mother and Father – for your love and guidance.
Thank you, Samantha and Taylour – for the joy that you bring.
Thank you, family and friends – for your encouragement.
Thank you, Marie – for your artistic talent and insight.
Thank you, Judith – for your keen editorial eye.
Thank you, André – for your expertise.
Thank you, Milt – for your dedication.
Thank you, Ramel – for your kind words.

Preface

Life is a trip. Literally. Life is a trip. It is a spiritual journey. This book is meant to be a guide for your spiritual journey. Read it with an open mind.

As you read this book, it is important to understand that I did not take a religious approach in the writing of it. Religion has to do with rules, regulations, limitations and historic conditioning. Having said that, I believe that all religion—regardless of its form—has at its core, a desire to be with and have a personal relationship with God, the Source, or whichever term you choose to use to refer to the Divine Infinite Spirit. Spirituality is a personal journey, but as the book explains, you don't have to go very far. In fact, when you decide to open the door to the possibility, you might discover that you don't have to go anywhere at all. When you decide to open the door to the possibility, you might just discover the divine within.

The idea for this book came to me in a moment of quiet meditation. I wrote it because all of my life I've had so many questions. Why are we here? What's it all for? What's the meaning of life? What's my purpose? And what's with all this pain? What's that about? Why? What? Why? My own journey has guided me to many different sources for the answers. I have listed some of them in the appendices. The sources that I list are not by any stretch of the imagination all-inclusive. They are just some sources of inspiration that resonated with me, spoke loudly to my soul, and have helped me in my personal journey.

Some of my questions have been answered, others I have yet to discover. One thing that I have discovered is that there is this light, this power within. It's there, but we don't *recognize* it. At first when you make this discovery, it may frighten you, but then it will intrigue you. And when you begin to learn more about it, you will begin to understand how it can bring you peace and joy. One source for this book was *Conversations with God*, which is actually a three-book series. In the first book, the author wonders, "How does God talk and to whom?" The answer is that God talks to everyone all the time, through books, music, movies, magazines, and a host of other venues, including life itself. The problem is that no one bothers to listen.

These words really resonated with me. And so I began to listen—really listen—to the words. And then I began to hear. What I heard spoke loudly to my soul... to my-*Self*. The result of these soulful revelations is a directory in the back of this book. It lists books, movies, music and other resources that contain easily overlooked, but valuable inspirational messages. Messages that when really listened to and heard, reach deep into the soul... into the Self. I have not read all of the books, nor have I visited all of the websites in the directory. However, if a resource appears that I have not read, listened to or visited, then I have either read the summary for it or it was referenced or recommended in one of the texts that I have read. I wanted to share as many resources with you that I could.

In addition, to more fully illustrate its points, you will see many quotes in this book. Some quotes give insights on more than one level, so you may see them in more than one place.

This book is a nonfiction work; however, you will find a few fictional anecdotes throughout the book that I have included for the purpose of example.

Finally, a supplementary companion journal that I call *Journal for your-Self* has been included as the very last segment of this book. *Journal for your-Self* has four distinct components: Letters of Forgiveness, Affirmations, Design for Your Life, and Creative Thoughts.

Letters of Forgiveness begins with two fictional letters to help you get started. It is followed by several empty pages. Use these pages to compose your own letters of forgiveness to people that you are having trouble forgiving. The intent is to give you the opportunity to purge your emotions, release that energy, get it—whatever it is—off your chest, so that you can let go and move on.

The second section of the journal is **Affirmations**. The intent of this section is to give you the opportunity to write down positive declarations and/or promises to yourself that you want to keep.

The third section of the journal is **Design for Your Life**. What if you could take out a pen and paper and design your life, not the way it is today, but the way you would like it to be? What would you write? What if after you answered this question, the world would around you said, "Okay," and responded accordingly. What would you write? **Design for Your Life** is reserved for you to answer that question. Once you answer it, read your answer aloud, every day.

The last section of the journal is **Creative Thoughts**. There are no rules or guidelines for this section. You can use this section to write whatever you want.

Finally, my spiritual quest has helped me to learn that part of our purpose here is to help others. So, we might do well to ask ourselves, "What can I do to help?" As a human being then, I asked my-Self that question. The answer to this question came in many forms—this book was one of them.

Peace and Joy Until You Reach the Light,
Valerie Rose

Dedication

*This book is dedicated to every soul
that's ever pondered the meaning of life.*

What people are saying about "You Better Recognize!"

"If life is a lesson 'You Better Recognize!' is the commencement speech you should've heard. If you've grown weary of an uninspiring religion, here's the sermon you missed. 'You Better Recognize!' is food for thought, so clean your plate."

Dennis Kimbro
Author, "Think & Grow Rich: A Black Choice"

"What a great testimony to the power of the human spirit! I recommend this book to anyone interested in personal development. It's a true guide to the pathway of recognizing and utilizing the greatness that lies within us all."

Desi Williamson, CSP
One of America's top motivational speakers, Author, "Get Off Your Assets!"

"As an author, consultant and motivational speaker, I believe that "You Better Recognize!" is packed with great inspirational messages and can serve as an important "lessons learned toolkit" to take with you along life's journey. Valerie's approach in "You Better Recognize!" invites personal growth and discovery."

Deborah A. Watts,
Author, "101 ways to know you're "black" in corporate america"
President, Watts-Five Productions

"My husband, Jeff, is helping me with the final proofing of the manuscript. He is so into this book that he keeps reading me passages from it. I keep telling him that I've ALREADY READ IT!! He said, 'I know. But, it's the kind of thing you want to share out loud.'"

Judith Hence, Editor
Henceforth, Inc.

A Note from the Author

Dream your dream.

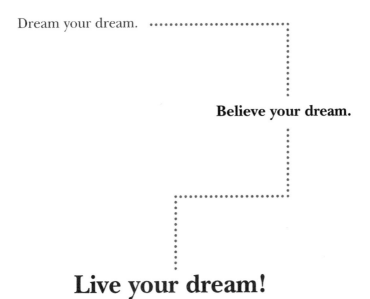

Believe your dream.

Live your dream!

"The mind is deep...deeper than you think."
– Valerie Rose

"We are not human beings having a spiritual experience;
we are spiritual beings having a human experience."
– Teilhard de Chardin

Self Discovery

Self discovery is only a matter of recognition.

The Road...

Recognition	Knowledge	Detection
Acknowledgement	Watchfulness	Unfolding
Awakening	Psyche	Disclosure
Mind	Wakefulness	Showing
Subconscious	Attentiveness	Unearthing
Cognizance	Subliminal Self	Finding
Awareness	Revelation	

To Self...

Energy
Pure Potentiality
Essence
Breath of Life
Sentience
Inner Glow
Soul
Spirit
Consciousness
Being
Inner Self
Silver Lining
Self
Espirit
Spiritual Being

Discovery...

Truth

RECOGNIZE
the light.

RECOGNIZE
the light in you.

On the light within:

> "What lies behind us and what lies before us are tiny matters compared to what lies within us."
> – Ralph Waldo Emerson

> "But the Secret sits in the middle and knows."
> – Robert Frost

> "Look within!... The secret is inside you." – Hui-neng

> "It is within you, that you can really be you."
> – Samantha Elayne, age 11

> "We have what we seek, it is there all the time, and if we give it time, it will make itself known to us."
> – Thomas Merton

> "The Kingdom of Heaven is within you... Seek ye first the Kingdom of Heaven and all things will be added unto you." – Jesus of Nazareth

"Mommy, where is God?"

"Mommy, where is God?"
"God is everywhere, baby."
"How come I don't see him?"
"Well, you might not be able to see him, baby, but God is

everywhere… in the flowers, in the trees, in the air… he's even here with us right now."

That's what our parents told us when we were children. Most of us let them off the hook and embraced the notion that "God is indeed, everywhere." It is a lovely notion and it's one in which many people, and I still believe. But the problem is that when most of us embraced this divine notion that "God is everywhere", the word "everywhere" seemed to entail anything and everything outside of ourselves. In other words, because we many times feel so weak and powerless in the face of life's circumstances, we believe that God is anything and everything, but us.

The American Heritage dictionary defines the word, **everywhere**, as: **In every place; In all places**. So if God is everywhere, it follows then that God is also in us. But as children, that point seems to have been lost with us. We missed that subtle nuance. And most of us are still missing it. But the reality is that the word "everywhere" is inclusive, not exclusive.

All things considered, if you believe that you were created by God.* If you believe that you were created by this Invisible Force of Energy and that this Force of Energy is everywhere, then it stands to reason that this Force of Energy is running through you. And since this Force of Energy is running through you, it's also running through every other living thing. And this Force of Energy, this Light, is in you and that means it's accessible. In other words, you can tap into this Energy through meditation, prayer and most importantly an open mind. And when you tap into it, you will understand that your potential is unlimited. In other words, nothing is impossible for you.

---

* God is known to different people by different names. Substitute whatever name or terminology that that you feel comfortable with.

When you get in touch with this Energy, when you connect with this Light that is waiting for you to discover that it is there, you will understand that you have the ability to create and rock your own world. So, the next time you sing that old familiar church hymn, "This Little Light of Mine," take those lyrics literally, and take heed. Be happy, be kind, be generous and people will recognize that light and be attracted to that light. Turn inward to get in touch with yourself. Turn inward to get connected with yourself.

Recognize that the universe is a powerful dynamic, all you have to do is to be open to its energy. How? You are the impetus. You are the key.

RECOGNIZE
that you are a powerful force
in the universe.

On creating your own destiny:

"It is a painful thing to look at your own trouble and know that you yourself and no one else has made it."
– Sophocles, Ajax, c. 450 B.C.

"You have to expect things of yourself before you can do them." – Michael Jordan

"We create our own destiny by the way we do things. We have to take advantages of opportunities and be responsible for our choices." – Benjamin Carson

Self Discovery

What if you could take out a pen and paper or sit at a computer and design your life, not the way it is today, but the way you would like it to be? What would you write? What if after you answered this question, the world around you would say, "Okay," and respond accordingly. What would you write?

"Zoe"

Zoe wants to design clothes. She has a gift for it, always has. Her mother was a talented seamstress who passed along her many skills to her daughter. Zoe's mother taught her to make everything from Halloween costumes to sequined prom dresses. She loved every moment of it. Late at night in her room, Zoe would spend hours drawing elaborate sketches of avant-garde fashions of her own design. She had plans to attend design school in New York in the fall, but her plans were derailed when she came home from school one day to find police cars and paramedics in the front of her home.

Meteorologists had warned the public to stay well hydrated if planning to be outside for any length of time, especially if engaged in any type of activity. But not only was Zoe's mother a wonderful seamstress, she was an avid gardener who had a zest of life. *Why in the world would she stay indoors on a beautiful day like today?* She wondered, leaving her water bottle sitting on the kitchen table.

When her mother died, Zoe was devastated. She had no idea that people could actually die from heat stroke. She had no choice but to give up her plans for school, so that she could work to take care of her father. Now that he's gone, she feels empty and numb because not only has she lost both of her parents, but she's stuck in a dead-end job with no prospects, no passion, and $15,000 in debt.

Scenario one: Woe is me
Feeling hopelessly disillusioned and despondent, Zoe calls her friend Eboni, a successful photographer, everyday to complain about her life. "Eboni, I hate my job." "Eboni, I hate my life." "Eboni, I'm so lonely. I don't have a man. No one loves me." "Eboni, I wanted to be a fashion designer, but so many years have gone by that I've lost my passion. I've lost my drive." "Eboni, I never have any money." "Eboni, I hate my hair." "Eboni, I hate my skin." "Eboni, I'm so fat." "Eboni, I'm so depressed. I just want to die." "Eboni, Eboni, Eboni…"

Scenario two: Taking Charge
Sick and tired of Zoe calling her every day to complain about her life, Eboni decides to take action. She gives her friend a book to read and makes her promise to read it. Not an avid reader, Zoe reluctantly agrees and takes the book home. Only a couple of pages into the book, she was about to toss it into the corner with the rest of the books that Eboni had given her when she came across the following lines:

What if you could take out a pen and paper or sit at a computer and design your life, not the way it is today, but the way you would like it to be? What would you write? What if after you answered this question, the world around you would say, "Okay," and respond accordingly. What would you write?

Zoe thought about the answer to this question and in the space that the author provided, she wrote the following:

I am one of the world's most sought after fashion designers. I am stunningly beautiful. Everywhere that I go, people tell me that I am stunningly beautiful. My man is passionately in love with me. In fact, I am surrounded by people who genuinely love me. I have lots of money. I'm wealthy, in fact. Everywhere that I go, my parents are with me in spirit. I can feel their guidance and direction. My life is full of joy and bliss.

Everyday after that, she pulled it out and read it aloud. She also decided to take up fashion design in night school. One year later, Calvin, Eboni's husband, learned that the pilot he'd written for a dramatic TV series got the nod from the network brass. The series took off and was nominated for two Emmy awards in the categories of Outstanding Drama Series and Outstanding Writing for a Drama Series.

Zoe started to cry when Eboni asked her to design her dress for the event. It was hard to juggle between work and school, but Zoe was passionate about it, working late hours into the night. She was working so hard that her boyfriend, began to complain that he never got to see her. But she was determined not to embarrass her friend in front of all of Hollywood. Sometimes she worked all the way through the night, even though she had to go to work the next morning.

Eboni fell in love with the dress that Zoe designed for her. When she wore it to the awards ceremony, she received many compliments from lots of different people, including the woman that she was seated next to. The series did not win an Emmy, but both Zoe and Eboni were pleased with the fashion statement that Eboni had made.

Six months later, Calvin asked Eboni if she remembered the woman who sat by them at the awards ceremony. It turns out that the woman that Eboni was sitting next to had recently been offered a position of power on a new television show. The series centered around an eccentric young woman and her wildly, unconventional friends. But wardrobe for the cast had been an issue from the beginning. In order for the story line to be believable, they couldn't just put the cast in anything. They needed something fresh, something new, something *avant-garde*... something like that dress that Calvin's wife wore to the awards ceremony last year.

Zoe left her 9 to 5 to design clothes for the new show. Young people all over the nation are still imitating her trend setting designs.

The above is a fictional account. I included it to illustrate a simple point: Your words have power. You have the power to change your reality because your words have power. If you begin the practice of reciting affirmations, you will notice a change. You might not notice anything right away, but you have to be aware, you have to be paying attention. For example, if you decided that beauty was the goal. If you practiced reciting the following: "I am stunningly beautiful. Everywhere I go, people tell me that I am stunningly beautiful." People will begin saying things like: "You know, I really like your hair that way." "You look different. What are you doing?" "You look stunning." These remarks in an everyday conversation can easily go unnoticed, but you have to be aware. You have to be paying attention.

Have you ever been around someone whose only conversation is about how depressed they are or how sick they are or how they hate their job or spouse? When you think about those people, it is probably true that they are depressed, sick or hate their jobs. Their spouses probably treat them such that yes, they do indeed hate their spouses. But what is more telling is that these people have created their own reality by speaking their reality into the universe on a continual basis.

You have responsibility for what you say. You are responsible for your words. Talk about what you do like. Don't dwell on what you don't like.

The universe is a powerful dynamic—that power is running through you. Speak your destiny into the universe and trust the universe to produce it in your reality. I know that might sound a little strange, but I know first hand that this can produce very real and tangible results.

"A Dream Come True"

Everyday on the drive to work, I would recite various affirmations. One of the affirmations that I would repeat over and over was: "I am a best-selling author and it's all going to start with the publication of *Cappuccino in the Winter.*" *Cappuccino in the Winter* was published by Avid Press in 1999. Not only had I moved my dream into my reality, but that dream opened doors for me that I never before thought possible. It's given me opportunities to go places, do things, and meet people that I never thought I would. And I have not given up my dream of being a best-selling author someday. In fact, I have no doubt in my mind that it too, will come to fruition someday. And when I make that statement, please don't mistake it for cockiness. Look at it for what it really is… responsibility taken for the ability to create my own reality.

"The Manicure"

My sister, Helayna (not her real name) and my two nieces
were coming up to visit me. So I decided to take them to a
spa in Stillwater, Minnesota, near the St. Croix River for some
"pampering." I called the spa to set up the appointments and
was told that they were all booked for the weekend, because
of Lumberjack Days.

I called back the next day and was told the same thing.
Refusing to take no for an answer, I called again a week later.
This time they had two pedicure appointments available, so I
booked them for my sister and niece. But my other niece
didn't want a pedicure, she wanted a manicure. I figured I
could just sit out. I called everyday after that with no luck.
The week before they were to arrive, I called the spa and
learned that they had an opening for a massage. Since my
niece didn't want a massage, I booked it for myself.

That weekend when my family arrived, I shared all the spa
details with them and explained that I was not able get a
manicure appointment. My niece said there was no problem,
but I was determined to get her a manicure. All that
morning I just kept saying, "They're going to have a
cancellation or something. Watch." Helayna just kept
looking at me, shaking her head.

"Val, I don't know why you keep calling them and saying
that. They said no. No means no."

"I'm telling you, they are going to have a cancellation.
Watch!" I said confidently.

When we arrived at the spa, I asked the woman behind the
desk if they had any cancellations, explaining that I was

hoping to get a manicure for my niece.

"No. I'm sorry. We're booked solid because of Lumberjack Days."

"Oh," I said, disappointedly.

My sister and niece went in for their pedicures while I went in for my massage. When my massage was over, I again went to the desk to see if they had any calls for cancellation.

"No. I'm sorry."

"Thanks." I went into the room where my sister and niece were getting their pedicures done and took a seat in one of the vibrating massage chairs. My other niece was sitting on the sidelines, watching the three of us, trying not to look pitiful, when the door swung open.

"Hi Nancy," Julie chimed.

"Hey, Jules."

"I thought you were coming in at one."

"Yeah, I did get here at one, but when I got here I found out my 1:00 had cancelled. So, I've just been hanging out until my 2:00 comes. I thought I'd come in here and see what you guys are up to."

My eyes immediately cut over to Helayna who was already looking at me. I tossed her a wink and a smile and went into my spiel.

"You know Nancy," I said, "my niece over there really wanted to get a manicure today. Do you think you could squeeze her in before your 2:00?"

"Sure. No problem," Nancy said, smiling.

I think this whole episode made Helayna a little bit nervous because the rest of that day, out of the corner of my eye, I would see her staring at me like she was trying to figure me out or something. Or maybe she was saying to herself, *Maybe Val hasn't gone off the deep end. Maybe there is something to this thing.* I'm not exactly sure what she was thinking, but whenever I caught her doing that, I would just laugh and say: "It's not just me, Helayna. It's in you too. The power is in all of us. We just have to recognize it."

Speak your truth and after a while, you will stop wondering if it will happen, but you will begin to wonder how and when it will manifest itself. It's worth noting here, however, that while you can expect the truth to manifest, it does not always manifest itself in the way you may expect it to. So expect the unexpected.

Recognize that while you have the power to create positive change in your life, you also have the power to create negative things. For example, there were times in my life when I was frustrated with my marriage. I didn't necessarily want to get a divorce, but still I would say things to myself and to others like: "I'm just gonna get divorced." Or "I'm getting divorced."

Understand that by focusing on the negative, you are cementing it into your reality. Your words are giving it density and thereby making it real.

"Sasha and Ronald"

Sasha and Ronald have a thing going on. Since one was always at the other's place most of the time anyway, they decided to move in together.

Ronald fell for Sasha because she was a sexy, intellectual who rejected him five times before she agreed to go out with him. That in itself, was intriguing and stimulating to him. Sasha had been on her own since the age of 14. He really admired her drive and independence. But now, two and a half years later, they can't even have a conversation without her sweatin' him about flirting with other women and about getting married. Not only that, but her sexy negligées have been replaced with t-shirts and bloomers. Geez, he wishes she would fix herself up more. Maybe if she did, he would pay more attention to her and she would get off his back about that too. Ronald has deep feelings for Sasha, but after a painful divorce, he ain't tryin' to jump the broom again. Maybe this whole thing was a mistake.

Sasha hated Ronald when she first met him. He was good looking and all, but his cocky arrogance made him completely unappealing. She only went out with him because he promised he would stop asking her if she did. But after their first date, she realized that all was not what it seemed and was hooked. Ronald, she discovered, was a genuinely warm person and a real charmer, a real southern gentleman. He would open doors for her, pull out her chair and bring her flowers for no reason at all. And most importantly, the man knew how to cook! But two and a half years is a lot of time to have invested in a relationship. She wants to get married and have children. But ever since she broached the subject, Ronald's been acting kind of funny. And sometimes, he acts like he's keeping something from her. She wishes he would be more open with her. And even though he assures her that he's just being friendly, she also wishes he would stop flirting with the waitresses when they go out to eat. But what can she do, he's not wearing a ring. He's not her husband, at least, not yet. She loves him, but if he's not willing to make a commitment, then she has no choice but to move on.

Ronald on the negative tip:
Ronald could expend his energies complaining to his buddies about how Sasha's sweatin' him about getting married. He could continue to criticize her appearance and raise his voice when he tells her to get off his back about the marriage thing. In which case, they would probably break up.

Ronald on the positive tip:
On the other hand, Ronald could take Sasha out to dinner to a nice restaurant where he would focus his attention on her completely. He could present her with a beautifully gift wrapped box that has a lacy, black negligee inside and tell her how beautiful she would look in it. Ronald could say to himself, my girlfriend is a stunningly beautiful woman. She is independent and secure in our relationship. This scenario will more than likely get him what he wants. Chances are, this time next year Ronald will be happily in the arms of the woman he loves.

Sasha on the negative tip:
Sasha could expend her energies by going on and on to her girls about what a flirt Ronald is, and how she loves him but how the man's got a commitment problem. Sasha could tell Ronald everyday about how her biological time clock is running out. She could stop keeping herself up, telling

herself all the time, *What's the use anyway, he's not going to marry me.* In which case, Ronald would continue to flirt with women and probably not marry her. But if he did marry her, he would eventually have an affair. And she of course, would fall apart and blame the whole thing on him for the rest of her life.

Sasha on the positive tip:
On the other hand, Sasha could spend her energies repeating to herself the following: I am a stunningly, beautiful woman. Everywhere I go, people tell me that I am a stunningly beautiful woman. Whenever we go out, men of all races stare at me. Even in the company of beautiful women, Ronald can't take his eyes off me. Romance is Ronald's middle name. Ronald is open and honest with me. I am going to be married to the man I love by this time next year. This scenario is more apt to get Sasha what she wants. Chances are, this time next year, Sasha will be married to Ronald (or the man that she loves) and expecting twins.

("Sasha and Ronald" is a fictional account by Valerie Rose)

"On the Radio"

Consider the following: You have your headphones on and you're jammin' to your favorite oldie but goodie on the radio. Suddenly, the reception starts going in and out. *The radio station has a problem,* is your first thought. *Geez, I wish they would get it together, they're messing up my song!* It never occurs to you—not even once—that the last time you changed the batteries, a different president was in office. The only thing that occurs to you is that the radio station has a problem. Look first to see what you are doing on your end that may be causing the problem.

Try something new. Try not to complain about things you don't like. Try not blaming him or her for what he or she did to you. Look to see what you can do differently. Focus on what you like. Not what you don't like. Take some responsibility for your own actions. Read the writings of Miguel Ruiz who wrote *The Four Agreements*. And Deepak Chopra, M.D. who wrote *How to Know God*.

Recognize that your words have power.

RECOGNIZE
that opening your mind can open doors.

On the solutions to problems:

> "Stop focusing on the problem. Look past the problem so that you can find the solution."
> – paraphrased from the movie *Patch Adams*

> "There's a Spiritual Solution to Every Problem."
> – Wayne W. Dyer (See the book listed in the appendix.)

What we used to believe and say:

> "The Earth is flat."
> "The sun revolves around the Earth."
> "Man will never fly to the moon."
> "People will never have personal computers on their desks."
> "People will never have computers in their homes."
> "Man will never go to the moon."

There was a time when all of these statements were accepted as indisputable, universal truths. Were it not for people with open minds and the courage to reject conventional dogma, these statements might still be unchallenged.

The only way for new ideas to flow into your mind is for your mind to be open to receive them. If your mind is closed, how can a new thought enter? Consider a new way of thinking. If your mind is closed, fresh ideas cannot enter into your world. Clear the way for new ideas. Consider the possibility, even if you don't agree with the concept—whatever it is— it's still a matter of education. New thinking leads to growth and evolution. Open your mind to a fresh, new way.

Recognize that an open mind is a creative mind, and a creative mind has unlimited potential.

RECOGNIZE
and acknowledge the inner you.

On the inner you:

"You have to know that your real home is within."
– Quincy Jones

"The way is not in the sky. The way is in the heart."
– Buddha

"Knowing others is wisdom, knowing yourself is Enlightenment." – Lao-Tzu

"We dance round in a ring and suppose, But the Secret sits in the middle and knows." – Robert Frost

"Look within!... The secret is inside you." – Hui-neng

"What lies behind us and what lies before us are tiny matters compared to what lies within us."
– Ralph Waldo Emerson

"I suppose what makes me most glad is that we all recognize each other in this metaphysical space of silence and happening, and get some sense, for a moment, that we are full of paradise without knowing it." – Thomas Merton

"I have a body and I am more than my body.
I have emotions and I am more than my emotions.
I have a mind and I am more than my mind.
I am a center of pure consciousness and energy."
– The New Living Qabalah (Kabbalah as arranged by Will Parfitt)

"Your vision will become clear only when you look into your heart... Who looks outside, dreams. Who looks inside, awakens." – Carl Jung

"Feed Your Spirit"

Just as plants, flowers and trees need nourishment and proper care to grow and flourish, so does your spirit. But your spirit does not thrive on water, sunlight, and nutrients from the Earth. Instead, nourishment for the spirit comes in the form of new information and quiet introspection. Without them, your spirit will cease to grow.

When you open your mind, you may open the door to a new way of thinking. When you open the door to a new way of thinking, you may unlock your true potential. When you unlock your true potential, it may well be the key to a new life.

"Recognize"

Self-discovery is only a matter of recognition. Take some time for yourself. Be quiet. Give your mind the freedom to develop a new idea.

Recognize and honor the energy that resides within. Get in touch with yourself and you will get in touch with your spirituality. Take time out for your spirituality and that energy will return to you in the form of many blessings.

Be thankful.

Turn inward to find answers to your questions. Educate yourself on new ideas, even if you don't agree with them.

Recognize that you better recognize.

RECOGNIZE
that you are love.

On love:

> "Our highest word, and the synonym for God."
> – Ralph Waldo Emerson

> "Friendship set on fire." – Jeremy Taylor

"The heart's immortal thirst to be completely known and all forgiven." – Henry Van Dyke

"Spiritual fire." – Emanuel Swedenborg

"Two minds without a single thought." – Philip Barry

"Love is what's in the room with you at the holidays if you stop opening presents and listen." – Bobby, age 5

"If you want to learn to love better, you should start with a friend who you hate." – Nikka, age 6

"Love is like a little old woman and a little old man who are still friends even after they know each other so well." – Tommy, age 6

"Love is when mommy sees daddy on the toilet and she doesn't think it's gross." – Mark, age 6

"You really shouldn't say 'I love you' unless you mean it. But if you mean it, you should say it a lot. People forget." – Jessica, age 8

Let your mind entertain the thought of an incredible energy so potent with love that it is almost unimaginable. Now recognize that this incredible energy runs through everything and everyone. Recognize that you can tap into it because you are everything and everyone.

We're all connected.

Recognize that your essence is love. Why do people talk about love all the time? We dream about it. We write about it. We sing about it. We make movies about it. We are obsessed with it. Why? Because it feels good? Because it's the best thing we have going on this planet? If you've ever been in love, you know the answer to that question is, "All of the above." You know love is an incredible feeling. So, if you're in love now – relish it, pleasure in it, appreciate it, but don't take it for granted.

Romantic love, however, is just one expression of love. Love can manifest in many forms: love for children, parents, siblings, family, friends, and pets. Whatever kind of love you are experiencing, express it and appreciate it. And remember, telling someone that you love them, takes on a different vibration than just letting them assume that you do.

Recognize that love is the best thing we have going.

RECOGNIZE
that there's a difference between religion and spirituality.

On beliefs:

"Do not believe in anything simply because you have heard it. Do not believe in anything simply because it is spoken and rumored by many. Do not believe in anything simply because it is found written in your religious books. Do not believe in anything merely on the authority of your teachers and elders. Do not believe in traditions because they have been handed down for many generations. But after observation and analysis, when you find that anything agrees

with reason and is conducive to the good and
benefit of one and all, then accept it and live up
to it." – Buddha

You can profess faith in any religion that you choose.
But if you have no faith in yourself, where does that
leave you? Let your spirit guide you. Connect with
yourself. Understand what's going on inside. Get to
know the *real* you. Get to know your inner self.

Recognize and honor your spirit.

RECOGNIZE
the blessing of forgiveness.

RECOGNIZE

that forgiveness is really a healing process
for you.

On forgiveness:

"People are often unreasonable, illogical and
self-centered; Forgive them anyway."
– Mother Teresa of Calcutta

"No man is rich enough to buy back his past."
– Oscar Wilde

"When I am able to resist the temptation to judge others, I can see them as teachers of forgiveness in my life, reminding me that I can only have peace of mind when I forgive rather than judge."
– Gerald Jampolsky

On bitterness:

"If I have learned anything in my life, it is that bitterness consumes the vessel that contains it."
– Ruben "Hurricane" Carter

"Bitterness imprisons life; love releases it."
– Henry Emerson Fosdick

"The Blame Game"

"He cheated on me!" "She cheated on me first!" Let go of anger and revenge. If you are consumed with bitterness, you are the one who's being hurt. You are the one who is not healing. When you hang onto anger and bitterness, it literally becomes a festering open wound.

If for example, a child falls, gets hurt, and runs home in pain, crying it would be understandable if that child chooses to stay indoors for the rest of the day. But if a year later that child is still upset and crying over that same incident, then that child's energy is being expended on the complaint. Everyone else is outside having fun, but because his energy is focused on the complaint, the child is missing out. The same is true for you. If you are whining and complaining about everything that goes wrong in your life, then your energy is being expended on negative things. What will you gain from it? While you are whining and complaining, everyone else is "outside having fun." So, who's losing out here? Take some time to put some salve on your wound. Maybe even go to bed early. But after that put a bandage on it and leave it alone.

Besides, incessant complaining about your problems is boring. People are bored because they don't really care. They have their own issues, and unless they're really close to you, they don't have the time or the motivation to get involved in your problems. Pretty soon if you persist in such negative behavior, they will see you coming and run the other way.

Forget about revenge. The Universe is a place of cause and effect. You reap what you sow. Let them deal with their own cause and effect. You need not get involved. Revenge is not productive. It's not productive because ultimately it is you who is losing out. Recognize that when you replace that kind of negative energy with forgiveness, you are freeing yourself.

If, on the other hand, you choose to hold on to feelings of hate, anger and revenge, your energy is then focused on negative matters. The inevitable result is a case of self-imprisonment. In other words, your soul is arrested. You are engaging in spiritually toxic behavior that prevents you from being free.

If you are consumed with bitterness, you are only hurting yourself, because you are reliving the incident—whatever it is—over and over and over again. Even worse, the person you're upset with probably couldn't care less. That person may well be pleased that you are killing yourself with anger and emotional pain. Do you really want to give that kind of power to someone? Wouldn't you rather have the control? The way you take control is to let go. This is not a lecture; I'm speaking from experience. I know this first hand, because before learning this lesson, I was the "queen of the grudges." Eventually, I realized that I was not hurting the person that I was angry with, instead, I was hurting myself by keeping the grudge alive. In order to keep the grudge alive, I was the one who had to think about it all the time. When I recognized this infectious pattern of behavior, I simply let go.

This scenario not only goes for others in your life; it goes for you, too. Forgive yourself. Free yourself. Give yourself some credit. Stop beating up on yourself. Recognize your accomplishments and learn from your mistakes.

"The Fire"

When I was about twenty years old, a company in Minneapolis offered me a summer internship. A close and dear relative (I'll call "Aunt Abby") graciously allowed me to live in an upstairs bedroom of her home during this time. I do not smoke now, but I did at the time, occasionally. One day, after finishing a cigarette, I crushed out the butt in an ashtray and tossed the contents into the trash. Later, I went downstairs to shower in preparation for a lunch date. When I'd finished showering, I climbed the stairs and was horrified to find the room engulfed in flames. To make a long story short, thankfully, no one was hurt. The firefighters put the fire out, but left a lot of damage in the wake. The insurance company, while they did do some repairs, did not do what they should have done. My Aunt Abby's home was never the same again. Never mind the intelligence factor, it suffices to say that this life episode was not a pleasant one for me.

As Minneapolis is now my permanent residence, from time to time I visit her home. I apologized for everything that happened. But with each visit the peeling plaster and stained drapes were constant reminders of the damage that was done by my hand.

For many years after I beat myself up over the incident. But I eventually realized there was nothing I could do about it. I couldn't go back and change it. What was done was done. I acknowledged my mistake, forgave myself, and moved on. Although the image is forever singed into my memory, I don't dwell on it.

Even though I have forgiven myself, I admit that I still question why it happened and why it happened to me. I'm not sure that I know the answer to that question, but perhaps it occurred so that I could recount the incident in this very book, in this very spot, so that you could read it in this very moment and possibly gain something from it. If that is the case, I hope that I have helped you or someone else.

Forgive yourself. It's okay to make mistakes. Forgive yourself, learn from the experience, move on to a new and better you.

"The Jacked Epidural"

When I was in labor with my first born, an orderly at the hospital asked me if I needed a wheel chair to get up to the delivery room.

"I think I can make it," I said, bravely (but foolishly) just before the next contraction hit. He stood there watching me. Unable to move forward, I crouched deeply in the knees and tried not to scream when what felt like a sledgehammer slammed into the lower part of my abdomen.

"You sure?" he asked, offering the chair and his services again.

Self Discovery

This time, I came to my senses and took him up on his offer.

I was pre-registered. The doctor left instructions that I was to be given an epidural upon my arrival. An epidural is a local anesthetic that is used, among other things, to block labor pain. The medicine is injected into the back with a very long needle.

I was in between contractions. The anesthesiologists, the nurses... everyone was screaming at me to be still so that they could stick this big, long needle into my back. It was terrifying. One minute the contractions felt as though they were tearing my insides apart and then when I would get through that, I would have people screaming at me to be still. But once the epidural was given, it was like heaven. I watched the monitor record my contractions, but I couldn't feel a thing. I could feel enough to push, though, and welcomed my first baby into the world.

Seven years later, I returned to the delivery room for the birth of my second child. This time I was begging for an epidural. They gave it to me, but this time, it only worked on left side of my body. I could feel all of the pain in the right side. I didn't know that a body could experience such pain. After it was over, I was so angry that I didn't give my second daughter a proper welcome into the world. The journey into existence is a long, long road. But, I didn't pick her up. I didn't hold her. All I could do was lay there and think about the pain that I had suffered and feel sorry for myself. In hindsight, I know what I did and what I should've done. But, I had to forgive myself and just try to move on from that event. Today, my little one is four and although I still think about what happened, I recognize that what is done is done and what is really important is how much I show her— now—that I love her.

Recognize that forgiveness is freeing.

RECOGNIZE

that not only is that person just like you,
but consider the possibility that in the
larger scope of reality, that person is
really just you.

"We are not human beings having a spiritual
experience; we are spiritual beings having a
human experience." – Teilhard de Chardin

Recognize that every person that you encounter is a human
being—just like you—trying to get through this wild
perplexing ride we call life—just like you. They are trying to
find their way—just like you. And chances are, they are not
at the same stage as you in the process. Life has a way of
pushing people to the brink. Just the idea of being dropped
on this planet with no information and no instructions is
enough to push one to the brink of madness. Confusion,
anger, fear… all of this surfaces at some point and time
when one tries to understand the purpose of life. But you
have to realize that not everyone is at the same stage at the
same time. People develop their own way of "coping."
So when someone's "coping" clashes directly with you, let
that person be. Let it go. That person will have to deal with
their own cause and effect at some point and time. Be busy
about keeping your cause and effect on the positive tip.

"The Connection"

I hug people a lot. That's the way I am. That's the way I grew
up. My family is very close, so it's just very natural to me. But
people are so disaffected when it comes to touching other
people, that they sometimes get the wrong idea. Sometimes

people think you are being sexual. It's a natural human instinct to touch, yet it's become almost taboo. It's a signal that we're all in this together. It's a natural human connection. I'm of the opinion that if we spent more time and energy in trying to connect with other people maybe we would discover the reality that we're all in this together.

"It's a Human Thing"

On the surface, it looks like we're all different. But the reality is that we are all the same. We are all human beings, who at some point and time in our lives, begin to wonder about the purpose of life. I used to think I was the only person wondering what this is all for – this thing called life. It's all so ridiculous. There had to be more to it. Then I realized we're all going through the same thing with the same questions: Why we are here? What we are supposed to be doing? What's with all this pain? What's up with that? We are all trying to figure out what it's all for. Each person will need to go within to find his or her own answers to those questions. There's something inside of each one of us that knows it wants to find God, but it doesn't know how to get there... at least right away. That's why this life is a spiritual journey.

Recognize humanity.

RECOGNIZE
yourself when you see yourself.

Many times that person who you can't stand, or that person who gets on your last nerve may be closer and more familiar to you than you realize or care to admit. If you look closely, you might see someone that you recognize. Consider the possibility that that that person is simply demonstrating to you, an aspect of yourself that you couldn't or refused to see before. Consider even, perhaps, that is you, demonstrating yourself to yourself.

Recently, I was having a disagreement with someone and when the exchange became kind of heated, I said something. And as soon as I said it, I recognized that someone else had said the very same thing to me as I was telling this person. And in that moment, I knew it was a healing. And I knew that I had made someone feel the exactly the way that I was feeling.

If you recognize yourself and you don't like what you see, then change it... in yourself.

RECOGNIZE
that to be accepting is to be loving.

On love:

> "Love is like a little old woman and a little old man who are still friends even after they know each other

so well." – Tommy, age 6

"It is wonderful how much time good people spend fighting the devil. If they would only expend the same amount of energy loving their fellow men, the devil would die in his own tracks of ennui."
– Helen Keller

You have a choice. You can be right, or you can be happy. Besides, your way is not always the right way. As long as it's not hurting you or anyone else, why not live and let live? Why? Because to be accepting is to be loving.

Recognize that life is a personal gift and tearing away the wrapping is half the fun.

RECOGNIZE
the light in others.

On others:

"How far you go in life depends on your being tender with the young, compassionate with the aged, sympathetic with the striving, and tolerant of the weak and strong. Because someday in your life you will have been all of these." – George Washington Carver

Rent the movie, *As Good As It Gets* to understand this more point more fully. All books, movies, and stories are about life on some level, but this movie speaks well to the subject and makes no apologies. It's one of my favorites because we can see how every human being has some redeeming quality, including those whom many may consider to be scum of the earth. When it comes to movies portraying life's crazy circumstances, *As Good As It Gets*, is as good as it gets.

By the way, this movie came on television as I was reorganizing the manuscript for this book. I knew this was no accident. When you elevate your awareness and open your mind, your perception shifts and you begin to recognize magic when you see it. What you assumed to be coincidence or a chance encounter might simply be the power of you made manifest. Open your eyes, be aware and pay attention.

Recognize the light in others.

RECOGNIZE
that life is change.

On change:

> "What the caterpillar calls the end of the world the master calls a butterfly." – Richard Bach

On life:

> "A little gleam of time between two eternities."
> – Thomas Carlyle

> "A play. It's not in its length, but its performance that counts." – Seneca

"Be here now." – Baba Ram Das

"Life is what happens while you are making other plans." – John Lennon

On the seasons:

"Spring passes and one remembers one's innocence Summer passes and one remembers one's exuberance. Autumn passes and one remembers one's reverence. Winter passes and one remembers one's perseverance." – Yoko Ono

On spring:

"A true reconstructionist." – Henry Timrod

On summer:

"Days dripping away like honey off a spoon."
– Wallace Stegner

On autumn:

"A second spring, when every leaf's a flower."
– Albert Camus

On winter:

"Trees stooping under burdens of snow, window filigreed with frost, shadows of drifting hummocks turning blue-cold as northerners mummify themselves in coats and scarves." – Henry Clayborne

Recognize that you're going to be okay because things do change. That's the way of the world. It's been said that nothing is constant except change itself. Nature makes this point each year in the change of the seasons. Everything must change. The white flakes of winter melt into the fertile womb of spring. The black soil gives birth to burgeoning green sprouts that mature and flourish in the warmth of the summer sun and burst into the burning colors of fall. When the colors have reached their peak, the leaves release their grip, fall and return to the Earth from which it came. Life is a rhythm. The seasons are symbolic for life itself.

Predictably full of surprise, that is life. Strange and familiar, that is life. Life is change. Life is a rhythm, a pulsating heartbeat. That's what life is. The opposite of a pulsation is a flat line. Flat line is a medical term that means dead. You are not dead. You are alive. You are life. You are love. Tell you something you don't know, right? Well, what you don't know, or perhaps, what you might not have paid attention to, is that life sans change is not really life at all. Life is change. If you get used to that fact, accept that fact, embrace that fact, then you can be at peace with that fact. When you are at peace with that fact, you can work within it.

Life is full of extremes. And extremes, when you look closer, are made up of the same elements. Ever heard that song, "There's a Thin Line Between Love and Hate"? Life is a rhythm that runs from one extreme to the other. Be at peace with that.

It's been said that life is a bowl of cherries... sweet but full of pits. Well, if that's true, relish in the sweetness of the cherry... and when you get to the pit, figure out what you're going to do with it. Are you going to choke on it, or are you going to use it to get some more cherries?

Life is amazing. Life is a blessing. Life is good. Focus on the good things in your life and keep moving forward. Instead of stressing, do something you like...

- If you have children, kiss their stubby toes.
- If you like to write—write!
- If you like to draw—draw!
- If you like to paint—paint!
- If you like to make love... make love.

Each time you engage in something you like, you are taking control. If you push your creativity to the foreground then your troubles have no choice but to move to the background, because the foreground will be filled with your joy.

"Ma"

My Mother is a wonderful, wonderful cook. But now that she is getting up in age, her body doesn't respond to standing in the kitchen for hours cooking the way it used to. As a result, she usually complains of leg and hip pain the next day and several days afterwards, and sometimes even weeks later. I don't live in the same city as my mother. I usually drive in when I visit. But when I do visit, my mother goes through a meal preparation routine that I usually try to talk her out of. I appreciate it, but when given the choice on consuming a home cooked meal and having her healthy, I would rather have her healthy.

When I drive in, I am usually tired and just want to relax. So in lieu of her cooking up a big meal, I tell her not to worry about me, that I can pick something up for all of us, or we can go out to dinner, or sometimes I cook something. But at some point during my visit, she insists on going through her routine. It used to be very upsetting to me. I felt it was such unnecessary work only to be in so much pain afterwards. Then I realized that my mother's "routine" was really giving her joy. That's when I relaxed, let go of my anxiety and decided to let her have her joy.

Life is joy. Bring some joy:

- Play Barbie with your three-year-old.
- Compliment your co-worker on her presentation.
- Give your man a full-body massage.
- Bake your mother a cake.
- Bring home a bottle of wine. Pour a glass for your wife and then ask her if you can paint her toenails. You will bring her joy. And afterwards trust me my friend, afterwards, she will bring you joy.
- Let your mother cook you a home cooked meal.

Recognize that change is life and life is a blessing.

RECOGNIZE
that it's a human thang.

On humanity:

"We are all citizens of one world, we are all of one blood. To hate a man because he was born in another country, because he speaks a different language, or because he takes a different view on this subject or that, is a great folly. Desist, I implore you, for we are all equally human. Let us have but one end in view, the welfare of humanity."
– Johann Amos Comenius

"Wherever there is a human being, there is an opportunity for kindness." – Seneca

"Be kind, remember everyone you meet is fighting a hard battle." – T.H. Thompson

"Beginning today, treat everyone you meet as if they were going to be dead by midnight. Extend to them all the care, kindness, and understanding you can muster, and do it with no thought of any reward. Your life will never be the same again." – Og Mandino

"It's a human thing, you wouldn't understand."

"It's a human thing, you wouldn't understand." Have you ever heard anyone say that? Unless it was said in jest, I would venture to say that the answer is "no." That's because, we are all human. We're all going through the same thing here. We're born, we go to school and graduate; we go to college and graduate; we get a job, get married, have kids, some of us get divorced, wait for retirement, and then we die. When we zoom in for a closer, more intimate view, it all seems so terribly urgent—getting that project done, getting the right grade, getting that promotion, getting that raise, getting that man, getting that woman. But by zooming out for a broader perspective, we can see the absurdity of it all. What if you died tomorrow? Would it be urgent then? Would it even be mildly important?

When you come to this realization, you begin to ask yourself some very pointed questions, like: "What am I doing here?" "What is my purpose?" "What's it all for?" "What is the point?" "What is the true meaning of life?" It is when you get to this point, that you begin to rouse from your sleep. Soon you will discover that the answers to your questions can only be found within.

I used to think it was just me, then I realized that we're all asking the same questions.

Recognize that each of us is on a mission of discovery and that the treasure can only be found within.

RECOGNIZE
the consequences of judging.

On judging:

> "If you judge people you have no time to love them."
> – Mother Teresa

> "Sweep first before your own door before you sweep the doorsteps of your neighbors." – Swedish Proverb

> "We should be lenient in our judgment, because often the mistakes of others would have been ours had we had the opportunity to make them."
> – Dr. Alsaker

As soon as you call that person stupid, ugly or an unfit mother, recognize that the Universe has a crazy way of conjuring up the exact circumstances that will make you feel exactly how you made that person feel when you made that judgment. It might not happen today or tomorrow, but at some point it will happen. And if you examine your own personal life closely you will recognize that.

Recognize the consequences of judging.

RECOGNIZE
the magic.

RECOGNIZE
the magic in you.

On appreciating miracles:

> "To be alive, to be able to see, to walk... it's all a miracle. I have adopted the technique of living life from miracle to miracle." – Arthur Rubinstein

> "Earth's crammed with Heaven."
> – Elizabeth Barrett Browning

"Isn't it amazing?"

Isn't it amazing how a little, tiny baby can grow, in some cases, from less than a pound into a full grown adult... literally, right before our eyes? How can the skin stretch and then all of a sudden just stop? When you think about it, when you *really* think about it, isn't that amazing. Really amazing? Yet, we never even notice it. We never even give it a second thought. We don't regard it with the wonder and amazement that it truly deserves. Because if you really paid attention to human growth from a baby to an adult, you couldn't help but be in total awe. But somehow the magic of this is lost on us. The sheer magnificence of it all is lost because we take it for granted.

We really should be in awe of such magnificence in ourselves, in each other, and particularly in our children, because we get to watch it all over again. That magnificence is you. That's you. That's the magic of you. Take some time to absorb and digest that. Do we really take the time to appreciate the incredible complexity of the human body? When we cut ourselves, our body goes right to work to repair the wound, usually leaving behind very little indication of an injury. The body can heal itself to new. That's amazing. That's really amazing. But, we take it for granted. We fail to see the magic in it. It really is amazing when you think about it.

Have you ever had an orgasm that felt so good, it almost hurt? That might read like an odd statement in an inspirational book such as this. But the truth is, sex is a normal, healthy, human experience that just happens at the same time to feel extraordinary. Mae West called it, "an emotion in motion." It is love being expressed.

Sex is something that should be enjoyed and celebrated. And what's more amazing, and magical even, is the creation of life that results from it. Isn't it interesting that from a human perspective, how men and women can be exactly the same yet physically and emotionally be so completely and totally different? There's magic inherent in that, but our fast paced lives let the magic float by unnoticed. The truth is that you are a stunning work of art. You are magic in the flesh.

Recognize the magic.

RECOGNIZE
that there is nothing wrong with being good to yourself.

On idleness:

"Take rest; a field that has rested gives a beautiful crop." – Ovid

"If you can spend a perfectly useless afternoon in a perfectly useless manner, you have learned how to live." – Lin Yutang

"Sit quietly, doing nothing, spring comes, and the grass grows by itself." – Zen Saying

"How beautiful it is to do nothing, and then rest afterward." – Spanish Proverb

"The time you enjoy wasting is not wasted time." – Bertrand Russell

"The Pleasure Principle"

You are still rousing to a full state of awareness. While you are making your journey, practice being nice to yourself. Take a long bath. Get a massage. Eat some chocolate. Take that trip!! Do something for you because you deserve it. Why deprive yourself of living? Isn't that what we're here for? As long as you are not hurting anyone, go for it. Indulge in a lively, guilt free session of sex for one. Eat some chocolate. Take some time out for yourself to do absolutely nothing at all.

If you're ever in Minneapolis/St. Paul, visit the Mall of America, and then you must visit SPA O.N.E. It's kind of like FUBU, in the form of a S.P.A. Black owned, it's a full service spa and salon that affirms and rejuvenates the spirit with its Afrocentric décor, and its sharp focus and dedication to its African-American women clientele. The "O.N.E" in Spa O.N.E. is an acronym for "our natural essence". What can I say—it's wonderful. Phone: 651-726-2407. Website: www.aromaat.com.

You may be asking why I chose to endorse Spa O.N.E in this book. Well, I am not related to the owner, if that's what you were thinking. But I felt it belonged in this book because it really is a wonderful way to rejuvenate the body and the spirit. After all, you're worth it right?

Whatever it is… Delight in it… Relish it… Luxuriate in it.

Recognize that you are worth it.

RECOGNIZE
that peace is within.

On taking time out:

> "Everyone is a house with four rooms, a physical, a mental, an emotional and a spiritual. Most of us tend to live in one room most of the time, but unless we go into every room, every day, even if only to keep it aired, we are not a complete person."
> – Indian Proverb

"In the Spirit"

Take some time for your spirituality. Meditate, pray, chant, recite affirmations, *be silent*, read spiritual books and magazines. Do whatever it is you do to stay in tune and be at harmony with your spiritual self. Use this time to reflect on you. Do it as often as possible.

Prayer, reading spiritual text, chanting and reciting affirmations are often choices that I make when I feel my spirit needs to be fed. But, more often, my tool of choice is meditation. It helps me to attain spiritual harmony and peace—it's sort of like a gas station for my spirit. Every morning when I get up to meditate, I feel like I'm refueling my spirit so that it can properly guide me through my day. When I don't meditate in the morning, I feel like I'm running around on an eighth of a tank of gas, and I'm forever worrying if I'm gonna run out. Meditation is also a coping mechanism that I use on a daily basis(along with the other tools mentioned) to help me to deal with the difficulties that life sometimes presents.

Carol Sydney's article in the May 2001 issue of *Open Minds* magazine says, "Meditation could be called the openness to experience what the five senses cannot detect." She further says that, "[It is] the heightened sense of awareness that leads us to the realm of the spirit."

"In My Zone"

To meditate simply means to think… to contemplate…to be aware, or to simply be silent. But, there are many different ways to meditate. How I choose to meditate depends on my mood, the weather, my location, and the time of day. Most days I wake up one hour before I have to get up and get ready for work; I sit in my bed and recite these three sentences over and over again: "I am peace." "I am joy." "I am light." Then I choose one of the sentences to focus on and repeat it over and over again. I choose the noun in the sentence and repeat that over and over again. For example: After repeating the three sentences, I might focus on, "I am joy," and the word "joy." After repeating it over and over, I sit in silence with my eyes closed, staring into the darkness, receptive to whatever.

"Jamaica"

In Jamaica, the sun has barely begun to make its way west. There is no reggae music and the sun-hungry tourists have not yet risen to greet the day. It's just me standing at the edge of a majestic blue sea that is always constant, yet, ever changing. The air is moist and tastes of salt. Overhead the birds rejoice in the freedom to fly and to just be. As the waves softly lap onto the shore, I marvel at the majestic beauty of the azure horizon and I blush as it rises to kiss the morning sun.

Sometimes I imagine myself being back there: I am at the foot of the Caribbean and it brings me peace.

"Black Hawk Lake"

Sometimes I take a walk around Black Hawk Lake. About three-quarters of the way around, I find a seat on a log bench. I tune my senses into nature's station and marvel at the sequined sunshine, as it shimmers across the water to meet the cascading ripples on the other side.

Recognize that spending time alone can bring you peace.

RECOGNIZE
the benefits of silence.

On silence:

"The fence around wisdom." – Hebrew Proverb

"True silence is the rest of the mind; it is to the spirit what sleep is to the body, nourishment and refreshment." – William Penn

"Liberty in tranquility." – Cicero

"Silence is more musical than any song." – Christina Rossetti

"Silence is our deepest nature, our home, our common ground, our peace. Silence reveals. Silence heals." – Gunilla Norris

"Yet it is in this loneliness that the deepest activities begin. It is here that you discover act without motion, labor that is profound repose, vision in obscurity, and, beyond all desire, a fulfillment whose limits extend to infinity." – Thomas Merton

"Everything has its wonders, even darkness and silence, and I learn, whatever state I may be in, therein to be content." – Helen Keller

Use this time to reflect on you. Use this time to reflect on your purpose. Use this time to put energy into pursuing your dream. Recognize your true potential.

When you are quiet, you might actually be able to listen to what someone else is saying. Not just hear it, but actually listen to it.

When you are quiet, your mind might bring you to an inspiration that could blossom into something special or something you didn't expect. This book, unexpectantly, came to me while I was quietly meditating.

When you are quiet, you might remember something that you had forgotten. I had planned to include this very point in this book, but I'd forgotten—that is until I was quiet—then it came back to me.

Recognize the magic in silence.

RECOGNIZE
that laughter is healing.

On laughter:

> "A smile that burst." – Patricia Nelson

> "A universal bond that draws all men closer."
> – Nathan Ausubel

> "A tranquilizer with no side effects." – Arnold Glasow

> "We shall never know all the good that a simple smile can do." – Mother Teresa

"Funny, you should ask."

It has been said that laughter is the best medicine. This statement should be taken seriously. Many, many documented cases bear witness to the healing properties of laughter.

Rent the movie, *Patch Adams*, starring Robin Williams.
Rent an Austin Powers movie.
Visit: http://www.rxlaughter.org/ and
http://members.aol.com/shrinkchat/humor.htm

As my three-year-old would say, "You better necked-nize!"

Universal Law

"Cause and effect."

"A balance of energy. Good for good. Bad for bad."

"For every action. There is a reaction."

"What you do comes back to you."

"You get out of the universe whatever you put into the universe."

"You receive from the world what you give to the world."

"Do unto others as you would have them do unto you." – Bible

"Every cause has an effect. Every action a consequence."

"Nothing is random."

"Love your neighbor as yourself." – Bible

"Do unto others as you would have them do unto you." – Bible

"As you sow, so shall you reap." – Bible

"You must sleep in the bed you made."

"You actions today define your future tomorrow."

"The chickens come home to roost." – Malcolm X

You are the creator of your own reality. At any given moment, you have a choice. You can at any given time choose to create positive energy or you can choose to create negative energy. It is through your energy choices that you create your own reality.

RECOGNIZE
Universal Law.

RECOGNIZE
and respect Universal Law.

On actions:

"We cannot live only for ourselves. A thousand fibers connect us with our fellow men; and among those fibers, as sympathetic threads, our actions run as causes, and they come back to us as effects."
– Herman Melville

"Everything you do, and everything you don't do, has an effect." – Kenneth & Linda Schatz

"In nature there are neither rewards nor punishments — there are only consequences."
– Robert Green Ingersoll

"If you see good in people, you radiate a harmonious loving energy which uplifts those who are around you. If you can maintain this habit, this energy will turn into a steady flow of love."
– Annamalai Swami

"Ignorance of the Law is No Excuse"

What is Universal law? What you do comes back to you. You get what you give. Why not start giving some joy and see what happens.

And what does that mean? Maybe that means paying off a bill that someone is desperately worried about and feeling the joy that resonates from your giving. Maybe it means making your Auntie some fried pies, simply because you know she loves them. Or maybe it means taking the time to give your three-year-old your full attention when she pointedly asks you if you are looking at her or at the TV. Maybe it means giving your ten-year-old your full attention as she recounts the events of her day. Or maybe it means calling someone's boss to tell him or her what a great job someone did for you. When we receive bad service, we can't wait to get to the phone or the PC to lodge a complaint. But, when we receive good service, we click the mute button. Next time, call someone's boss and say, "Hey, you know, this person really did a nice job for me, and I just wanted to let you know." Believe me, that energy comes back to you. I know. I've experienced it.

And by the same token, when you treat people badly, don't be surprised if people treat you badly. It may not happen right away, but it will happen. It may even happen in another life, but when it happens to you in this life, you will do well to ask, "Now what have I done to cause this?" In that way it will become a learning process in the evolution of a new and better you.

RECOGNIZE

that when you put negative energy into
the Universe, that energy at some point
and time will come back to you.

On consequences:

> "Life does not require us to be consistent, cruel,
> patient, helpful, angry, rational, thoughtless, loving,
> rash, open-minded, neurotic, careful, rigid, tolerant,
> wasteful, rich, downtrodden, gentle, sick, considerate,
> funny, stupid, healthy, greedy, beautiful, lazy,
> responsive, foolish, sharing, pressured, intimate,
> hedonistic, industrious, manipulative, insightful,
> capricious, wise, selfish, kind or sacrificed. Life does,
> however, require us to live with the consequences of
> our choices." – Richard Bach

"The Unjust Accusation"

I can remember when I was about 12 or 13 or something like
that, I was with a friend and I walked out of a music store
with a 45 record in my hand. I was walking and talking with
my friend when I realized that I had this record in my hand.
I immediately turned around to return it, but by that time,
the manager was on her way to get me—I got into a lot of
trouble and everyone thought I was a thief. It didn't matter
that I had more than enough money to buy this record. This
bothered me for many, many years, and finally, I asked God
to tell me why this had happened to me, why I had been so
unjustly accused. And I don't remember if it happened right
then and there, but I became aware of an incident that had
happened in my childhood. I might have been 8 or 9. My

family had been planning a surprise birthday party for me and somehow, they got it into their heads that this girl (I'll call her LaDonna) had told me about the party and ruined the surprise. When they asked me about it, I told them that she hadn't. They asked me again and again; each time I said, "No." They kept insisting she had. Again and again, they insisted that she had told me. Eventually, I just agreed with them, that she had, indeed, told me about the party. I'm not proud of that incident and I'm not exactly sure why I lied like that. But, in the end, she was unjustly accused. Just as I had been unjustly accused years later at a record store. What I know now and didn't know then was that cause and effect was being played out.

You have the power to choose how to expend your energy. I could have chosen differently. But, since I chose to lie, I caused someone to be unjustly accused. As a result, I was feeling the consequences of my action, even though it was several years later. The point I'm making here is that you have the power to choose, and you will experience the consequences of that choice, good or bad.

In essence, when you wrong someone, it's going to come back. Remember and recognize that.

Here's another example:

"The Lunch and the Promise"

Not long ago, I was in a job I didn't like; my supervisor, Nancy (not her real name) and I did not see eye to eye on anything. She did not like me, for whatever reason. Some of my issues with her were related to a promise that she had made to promote me if I moved to her group. She reneged on that promise. But, you must understand that Universal law is always at work.

The number of African-Americans where I work is relatively small. So, we usually organize a goodbye lunch for anyone leaving the company. It happened that a woman in this group, Erika (not her real name) was leaving the company. I hadn't heard anything about a good-bye lunch, so I called her up and asked if anyone had set one up. She said, "No," so I squared a date with her, sent out the invitation, and made all of the arrangements.

At the lunch, I happened to mention that I would like to get into technical writing. So, Erika mentioned that her department was looking at beefing up the documentation and training group." She gave me the woman's number to call and I was hired. That was about four years ago; I am still in that group and if I had to work at this same company, I don't believe I could be in a better group or work for a nicer supervisor. It's worth noting here that I had been trying to make the transition to a documentation and training group for the longest time. It's also worth noting that Nancy, my previous supervisor, was offered—and accepted—a job in another department. Shortly afterward, the company downsized and her new job was eliminated. When she tried to return to the old department the newly hired manager did not want to work with her. She was out of a job. It's also worth noting that one day I saw her in the hall and I told her that I was sorry and that I just realized that she has her way of doing things and I have mine.

Both of these stories illustrate the principal dynamics of Universal Law at work. Nancy was the cause of my negative experiences and she, in turn, experienced those same feelings based on the same set of circumstances.

I released positive energy by taking the initiative to organize a lunch for a co-worker's departure. I, in turn, received positive energy in the form of a new job.

Do you see how it works? What you put into the Universe is exactly what the Universe gives back to you – only more.

RECOGNIZE
that if you practice being generous, generosity will be practiced on you.

On generosity:

"Plant a kernel of wheat and you reap a pint; plant a pint and you reap a bushel. Always the law works to give you back more than you give." – Anthony Norvell

"Sow much, reap much; sow little, reap little." – Chinese Proverb

"Look around for a place to sow a few seeds." – Henry Van Dyke

"A handful of pine-seed will cover mountains with the green majesty of forests. I too will set my face to the wind and throw my handful of seed on high." – Fiona Macleod

"Boomerang"

What you put into the Universe is exactly what the Universe gives back to you – only more so. When I speak of generosity, I am not just talking about money. Be generous with your time, resources, energy, and love, as well. Not only will it make you feel good, but that energy will return to you at some point and time in the future.

Recognize that when you are generous, there are two beneficiaries.

RECOGNIZE
that we're all connected.

On being connected:

> "Only when one is connected to one's own core is one connected to others... And, for me, the core, the inner spring, can best be found through solitude."
> – Anne Morrow Lindbergh

"The Connection"

We are all connected. The only way to really understand this principal is to start by connecting with yourself.

Recognize that we are one.

RECOGNIZE
that you are asleep.

"Life is a dream"

> "We are not human beings having a spiritual
> experience; we are spiritual beings having a
> human experience." – Teilhard de Chardin

> "My father says that almost everyone is asleep...
> There are only a few people who are really awake.
> And those people live in a constant state
> of amazement." – paraphrased, Meg Ryan in the movie
> *Joe Vs. the Volcano*

"Wake Up"

Life is a growth process. Our spirit is growing and our
experiences define our processes. Life is a dream sleep in
which we are rousing to an awakening. Our experiences
keep trying to wake us up, but because we're in a deep sleep,
we keep hitting the snooze button. Until we are fully awake
and fully aware, we will continue to create the experiences
that are necessary in order to bring ourselves to a complete
state of awareness.

Recognize that your experiences are steps in the process of a
gradual dawning. When you begin to awaken you will begin
to understand that life is a dream experience – a brilliant
illusion. Maybe a big part of our purpose here on the planet
is to make this simple discovery.

Recognize that life is just an illusion.

RECOGNIZE

that by changing your attitude,
you can change your world.

On attitude:

> "Your living is determined not so much by what life
> brings to you as by the attitude you bring to life; not
> so much by what happens to you as by the way your
> mind looks at what happens. Circumstances and
> situations do color life but you have been given the
> mind to choose what the color shall be."
> – John Homer Miller

"Choices, Choices"

You are the architect of your life. You and no one else. You
always have a choice about how to be and react in any
situation. In other words, "stank" is a choice. You can choose
to throw "stank" in someone's face, but recognize and
understand that if you do, you are virtually guaranteed that
they will throw it right back.

You can, however, choose differently. Kill is a strong word,
but my mother always says you can kill a person with
kindness. Try it sometime. The next time your olfactory
senses are offended by someone else's attitude, try
something new. Try something different. Be cordial,
gracious, humble, and just smile and act as though they had
just given you the highest compliment. It does take some
conscious effort, but try it anyway, just to see what will
happen. It could prove to be a learning experience for the
both of you. It's possible that that person will "recognize",

clear the air, and alter the exchange between the two of you all together.

Recognize that "stank" is a choice, but you can choose differently.

RECOGNIZE
that if you don't take control, if you don't believe in yourself, no one else will.

On taking control:

> "The thought you have now shapes your experience of the next moment. Practice shaping the moment."
> – Tom Barrett

> "It may take practice to think more positively and more compassionately, but just as you must train a puppy to behave the way you want it to, you must train your mind to behave itself. Otherwise, like the puppy, your mind will just make a lot of messes."
> – Tom Barrett

"Affirmative Action"

Move away from negativity. Get in touch with the inner you. Recite positive affirmations everyday and believe them. Be in harmony with the affirmations that you recite. Walk through your life like you believe the affirmations that you recite. For example, if you make the following affirmation: "I am going to do what I said I would do." Be true to that. Let your life reflect that harmony. Be the cause and the effect will follow.

Recognize that you are the architect of your life.

RECOGNIZE
that gratitude is a path to happiness.

On gratitude:

> "There is a calmness to a life lived in gratitude, a quiet joy." – Ralph H. Blum

> "If you haven't all the things you want, be grateful for the things you don't have that you wouldn't want."
> – Unknown

> "Gratitude unlocks the fullness of life. It turns what we have into enough, and more. It turns denial into acceptance, chaos to order, confusion to clarity. It can turn a meal into a feast, a house into a home, a stranger into a friend. Gratitude makes sense of our past, brings peace for today, and creates a vision for tomorrow." – Melody Beattie

> "There are no mistakes, no coincidences. All events are blessings given to us to learn from."
> – Elisabeth Kubler-Ross

"He is a wise man who does not grieve for the things which he has not, but rejoices for those which he has." – Epictetus

"I had the blues because I had no shoes until upon the street, I met a man who had no feet."
– Denis Waitely

"Happy Days"

Some people recommend keeping a daily journal of things for which you are thankful. You know that feeling you get on Thanksgiving when you realize how truly blessed you are. You can have that everyday, if you choose. I do not keep a journal, but I do try to consciously remind myself of the good things in my life on a regular basis. This is one way to happiness.

The key to happiness is being happy. Just be happy. Be happy with your life now. This is not to say that you should give up on your dreams; by all means dream your dream. Believe your dream. Pursue your dream. But don't let that stop you from appreciating the life you have now.

Recognize that you have a lot to be thankful for, so be happy about that.

RECOGNIZE
that financial freedom is possible.

On becoming a business owner:

> "I am a woman who came from the cotton fields of
> the South. I was promoted from there to the
> washtub. Then I was promoted to the kitchen cook,
> and from there I promoted myself into the business
> of manufacturing hair goods and preparations."
> – Madame C. J. Walker

"All About the Benjamins"

If you had told me ten years ago that someday I would be a
business owner, I would have laughed. Yet today, I am just
that, a business owner and I wouldn't have it any other way.

Recognize that financial freedom is possible. Recognize that
financial freedom is not only possible, but it is also accessible.
But possibility and accessibility do not mean that it's just
going to fall out of the sky with no effort from you. It's
gonna take some work. Case and point: it is 1:27 AM as
I type this. (It was 4:28 when I finally went to bed.)
I recognize that financial freedom is possible. I recognize
that financial freedom is accessible. And because I believe it
is possible and accessible, I am willing to put forth the effort
to achieve it. The first big step to opening the door to
financial freedom is to open your mind to it.

The second step to opening the door to financial freedom is
to get some education. Find someone who's been where you
want to go. Find a mentor and pick his or her brain. If you

can't find a mentor, do some research on your own. Take some time to get some education. Learn about investing. A good place to start is NAIC.

NAIC (National Association of Investors Corporation) is an organization that helps beginners learn about investing. Go to their website and request an information kit and a free copy of Better Investing. NAIC's website: http://www.better-investing.com/

Do you know what a DRIP account is? DRIP means Dividend Re-Investment Plan. A DRIP account allows you to buy stocks without having to pay a stock broker a commission fee. Most companies have them. You buy one share of stock via a broker and pay the commission fee. After that you call the company and tell them that you are a stockholder and you would like to open a dividend re-investment account. Once your account is open, you can invest directly without going through a broker and without paying a broker's commission fee. Every month, the company will send you a letter asking you if you want to invest some money in the stock that you bought. If you do, you simply write a check, put it in the envelope and drop it in the mail. It's as simple as that.

If you're renting an apartment for $850 a month, you could probably get a house for that. When you own your own home, you can get a tax write off on the interest, which automatically raises your financial status because more money is in your pocket instead of Uncle Sam's.

Have you ever thought about owning your own business? Be open to the possibilities.

What's your credit like? Find out. Contact the credit bureaus to order a credit report.

For book references, credit bureau contacts, and other resources in opening the door to financial freedom, see the Financial Freedom directory in the Resource section of this book.

Recognize that financial freedom is both possible and accessible.

RECOGNIZE
that visualization can be a powerful tool in making your dreams come true.

On visualization:

"Most of us visualize on a daily basis, but we often do it unconsciously and in a negative fashion. It is called worrying. What happens to our bodies when we worry? We tense up, disrupt our normal breathing, and psycho-physically prepare ourselves for failure. Instead, learn to use positive visualization to prepare yourself for success. As you do you will transform the energy that supports your worrying into fuel for making your dreams come true."
– Michael Gelb and Tony Buzan

"Some men see things as they are and say why; I dream things that never were and say why not."
– Robert Kennedy

Universal Law

"The Grape Vineyard"

I sometimes imagine myself walking peacefully in an olive garden or grape vineyard, and I attain a certain peace. (I wrote the line you just read approximately six months before the rest of this section.)

On the return drive to Milan, near the end of my vacation in Italy, I began to feel a little down. While it had been a wonderful vacation, I still felt something was lacking. I had come all the way across the ocean and I didn't get to walk through an olive garden. Then I had an idea. I flipped through my English/Italian dictionary and looked up the words, olive and vineyard. I tried to explain to the driver that I wanted to stop and walk through an olive vineyard. My Italian was not exactly fluent. Okay, it was terrible. But he did understand the two words, olive and vineyard. He waved his arm and in broken English, I understood him to say that the olive vineyards were in the mountains or country side and that we were now in the flat lands, near the city... or something like that.

So then I looked up the word *grape* and tried to explain that I would like to walk through a grape vineyard. But he didn't understand. He thought I wanted to go to a winery and drink some wine. I didn't want to drink wine or go to a winery; I just wanted to have the experience of walking through a vineyard in Italy, because that's what I had visualized.

His wife, he told me, speaks English. So he got her on the cell, explained the situation to her and then handed the phone to me. I told her that I just wanted to walk through a grape vineyard, and then I handed the phone back to him. He spoke to her for a moment.

"Ah...," he said, smiling.

The next thing I knew, I was walking through a grape vineyard, just like I had visualized. I told my niece to take my picture. I didn't tell her, but I wanted that picture to be my personal reminder of the power of visualization.

Where do you want to go? What do you want to do? Let your mind take you there.

Recognize that your mind is a powerful tool to use in the attainment of your dreams.

RECOGNIZE
that you are an inspiration.

On role models:

> "The most important role models in people's lives, it seems, aren't superstars or household names. They're 'everyday' people who quietly set examples for you — coaches, teachers, parents. People about whom you say to yourself, perhaps not even consciously, 'I want to be like that.'" – Tim Foley

> "Some of the most important people in my life would be shocked to learn that they were role models. They weren't celebrities, or even particularly accomplished. But they had some quality that I admired, that made me want to be like them."
> – Donn Moomaw

"You don't have to know people personally for them to be role models. Some of my most important role models were historical or literary figures that I only read about — never actually met." – John Wilson

"Somebody's Watching You"

Whether you like it or not, somebody is watching you and that "thing" that you're doing, whatever it is. That thing can be positive or negative, but understand that people are watching you. They are thinking if you can do that, they can, too. I learned that lesson when a woman co-worker told me that she was talking to an editor about publishing her book.

"I Am Other People!"

I was chatting with a woman I hadn't known for very long when somehow the conversation moved to the subject of writing a book and getting published. She started telling me how she was talking to this editor at a local press house who liked her work. Suddenly, it occurred to me that the reason why my dream of writing a novel was a nebulous one, was that because subconsciously, I'd always thought that writing novels was something other people did. Now here was this person who, just like me, was an African-American woman, working an everyday job in the same company, trying to make a living. Here was this average, everyday, African-American woman telling me how she was talking to editors and publishers! That was a turning point for me because suddenly I realized that I am "OTHER PEOPLE!" In that defining moment, I got it. I understood for the first time, what a significant impact a role model can have in the life of a young person of color. You see someone who looks like you, doing things that you thought only other people did. Then you think to yourself, "If they are doing that, I can too!" Inside of a moment, a dream can go from the intangible to the tangible. In my case, a nebulous dream went from cloudy to crystal clear.

That woman was an inspiration to me.

"A Stunning Moment"

And then something else happened... While browsing the paperback section in a store one day, looking for Sidney Sheldon's latest novel, I was stunned to see what appeared to be an African-American couple embracing on the cover of a book. The pastel coloring of the illustration was a muted blue-gray, so I moved closer, still unsure. *It was arguable,* I thought, but I think they're Black. I picked up the book and studied it closely. *They are Black! The people on the cover are Black!* I remember standing in the store, dumbfounded, like I had just seen a ghost or something. Eventually, I regained my senses and purchased the book. In case you're curious, the book was *For Always* by Bette Ford, published by then Kensington, Arabesque, now BET Books. That author was an inspiration to me.

After that, I proceeded to have my book published. But even after having had such experiences, I don't know why, but I was shocked when the first person came up to me and told me that I was an inspiration to her. *Little ol' me... Why me? All I did was write a book.* Since that first time, others have come up to me with similar comments. But now I look back on it, and after having given it some thought, I understand why.

It doesn't matter if that "thing" that you're doing is good or bad, you are still an inspiration. People will try to do what you do. But remember, the choice is yours on what kind of inspiration you are going to be. Know and recognize that people are going to want to follow in your footsteps.

If you can motivate another human being to be a better human being, then you have tremendous power. If you can open that door... tap into that light... tap into that stream of consciousness... spark that emotion... ignite that flame... that fire in a person to make them want to be the best person that they can be, then you will recognize that you have tremendous power.

Recognize that you are an inspiration.

RECOGNIZE
the power in prayer.

On prayer:

> "Call on God, but row away from the rocks."
> – Indian Proverb

> "God gives every bird his worm, but He does not throw it into the nest." – Swedish Proverb

Recognize... that accessing the power within means employing no doubt.

"The Miracle Staircase"

While vacationing in Santa Fe, New Mexico, I visited a tiny chapel that was a very popular tourist site. It is the home of a one-hundred-year-old miracle – a spiral staircase in the center of its base. The story of the spiral staircase is that before it was built, the only way the choir members could get to the loft to sing was to climb a rickety, old ladder. Because many of the choir members were up in age, the climb was dangerous. Many of the elderly choir members refused to use the ladder. The nuns came together in prayer, seeking an answer. Shortly afterward, a man came out of nowhere and built this beautiful spiral staircase with only a saw, a hammer, and a giant tub of water. He did not even use any nails! When he had completed the staircase, he simply disappeared. No one knew who he was or where he came from.

You can read a more detailed account of this miracle at http://www.the-strange.com/staircase.html.

When I first heard this story, I thought, *What an amazing, wonderful miracle.* What I didn't know then and what I know now is that miracles like this one are accessible to each and every one of us at any given moment.

"The Jamaica Hotel Rooms"

A couple of years ago, I went to Jamaica with my sister and my two nieces. We were so excited and couldn't wait to get there. Our imaginations were overrun with all of the luxuries and pleasures that we were sure to receive upon arrival. But when got there, instead of a luxurious hotel room, we were given what looked like a bad motel room and it was on the ground floor. Words to the wise: never stay on the ground floor when visiting the Tropics! There were bugs in the bathroom. They were tiny, but they were bugs. It was just unacceptable. First, we complained among ourselves, then we joined hands and we prayed. Our prayer? "We thank you God, for what you have already done."

When we finished praying, we went to the lobby and talked to the manager about a room change. The manager would not cooperate and came up with all kind of excuses. So, finally, one of my nieces said something like, "Can we just go home then? We just want to go home."

The manager was still reluctant, but after she said that, he did send Michael, the reservation clerk, to show us some different rooms on the top floor. We went to at least 3 different rooms; and amazingly, each one of the rooms was "occupied" and the occupants were "busy". Michael told us to wait while he tried to find some keys for some empty rooms. When he returned he showed us this beautiful, ocean view suite on the top floor. There was room for all four of us in the suite so we said, "We'll take it." Later, we learned that Michael got into a little trouble with management. Apparently, there was some kind of mix up and Michael should not have shown us that room.

A year later, I returned to the same hotel with my sister and my daughter. We requested the same suite. Again, we were given a suite on the ground floor. To make a long story short, it, too, was unacceptable. Again, we joined hands in prayer, "We thank you for what you have already done."

We made our way to the lobby to again speak with the manager. The manager was again uncooperative. This time it was because all of the rooms in that section of the hotel were under going renovations. For these reasons, the manager explained, it really would be impossible for us to stay in those rooms. I forget what happened exactly, but all of the rooms in that section were indeed under going renovations – all of them, *except one.* The same suite that we had the year before had just been completed. Our room was changed and everything was fine.

"The Gala Event"

I was invited to do a book signing in the Author's Pavilion at the Congressional Black Caucus Foundation. While registration was included with the invitation, ticketed events such as the Prayer Breakfast and the Gala Event were not. The Gala Event was a formal, black tie, awards banquet that featured entertainment. It was the culminating event of the conference, and it was (as I quickly learned) an event not to be missed. This created somewhat of a problem for me, as I did not have a ticket and therefore, could not go. So you know, without a doubt, I was on a mission.

My first order of business was to speak my truth into the Universe. So, I said: "I thank you God, for what you have already done." (I learned that from *Conversations with God*) After that, it was on.

I went to the ticket office and told them that I would really like to go to the Gala Event. Notice that I didn't say, "I would really *want* to go," I said: "I would really *like* to go." There's a difference. One produces a state of wanting the tickets. The other produces the experience of receiving the tickets. At any rate, I was told that the tickets were sold out and that I should go to room 6. So, I went to room 6. I repeated my request and was again told that the event was sold out. I then asked if there was any way that I could possibly get a ticket. Again, I was told, "No."

I decided to at least get a ticket for the Prayer Breakfast. So, I went back to the ticket office and purchased a ticket for the Prayer Breakfast. By that time I was on fairly friendly terms with the ticket agents, so I asked one of the women if *they* had any ideas on how I could get a ticket to the Gala Event. She thought for a moment and then suggested that I might be able to work something out with one of my state representatives.

"That's a wonderful idea!" I told her, gleefully.

I rushed to an open couch on the concourse, opened the directory, and scoured its listings, looking for Minnesota representatives. It suffices to say, there were none. Next.

Then I thought that maybe the coordinator of the Author's Pavilion would have some ideas. He said the only way that he knew of was to be a volunteer; he gave me the volunteer coordinator's name and directed me to room 7. When I got to room 7, I explained to the volunteer coordinator how I would really like to go to the Gala Event; I asked if she could use another volunteer. Her response was not exactly encouraging.

Okay, what about the sponsors in the exhibit hall. They must have tables. Maybe one of them has some extra tickets. Refusing to give up (even though my feet were beginning to hurt) I trekked through the Exhibit Hall asking every major exhibitor if they had a table or an extra ticket. Again and again, I was told no.

Although, two exhibitors told me that I should just get dressed and show up, that's what they were planning to do.

By 8:00 p.m. I was tired, hungry, and still ticketless. I went down to the hotel restaurant to grab a bite to eat. That's where I met "Emma." Unlike me, Emma was a Washington insider. Not *all* the way inside, but inside enough to have some connections. Emma was also trying to get some tickets, she told me she would try to get one for me, too. We exchanged contact information.

I woke up Saturday morning, still ticketless, but still on a mission. I got dressed and made my way over to the Prayer Breakfast. I was seated at a table with two young women, Angie and Lisa (not their real names). Angie and I chatted a lot and developed somewhat of a rapport. After breakfast, I went to the ladies' room. Upon my return, Angie told me she saw her cousin up front and invited me to join her at his table. I agreed. After the breakfast, Angie asked her cousin (a congressman) if he could secure two tickets for us to attend the Gala Event. While she was doing that, I introduced myself to Ron and Copeland (not their real names), friends of the congressman, who were also sitting at the table. A little while later, after Angie had rejoined us, her cousin walked up and handed Angie *one*—as in *single*—ticket. Now, I was beginning to feel ill. I asked him if he was he *sure* he didn't have another one. His response was not encouraging. After witnessing this, Ron and Copeland encouraged me to just show up. They said I should just come with them. Reluctantly, I agreed. It was 3:00, the banquet started at 7:00, and I was still ticketless.

It was around 3:30 when I got back to my hotel room. The message light on my phone was flashing. The message was from Emma. I called her back only to learn that she still hadn't had any luck getting the Gala Event tickets. She was still waiting to hear from her contact. We talked to each other several times before she called one last time to tell me that she had not heard from her contact and that she was tired and was just going to go home. That was about 6:00, I think. Before she hung up, I told her about how so many people had told me to just show up and asked for her advice on this. She said, "I wouldn't do that if I were you." I thanked her, and hung up.

Forever the optimist, the little voice in my head whispered, "Not to worry. Just take a shower. It will save you time when it's time to get dressed. Then I looked at the clock. It was 6:30. Time for a reality check.

Okay. I'm not going. So what. It's just a banquet dinner. The world is not going to end if I don't go. I picked up the phone and called Copeland. I told him point blank, "Look, I'm not going over there with no ticket, 'cause I ain't trying to get my face cracked." He said he would really like to see me over there. I told him that was nice, but I was not going over there without a ticket.

It was 7:00 p.m. and my self-pity had developed into a serious Cinderella complex. Everyone was going to the ball, *except me.* The room was dark and the bed was sinking in from the weight of my disillusionment, when the phone rang. I answered the phone and looked at the red LED display on the clock: it was 7:15. It was Copeland, "You dressed?"

"I told you I'm not going over there without a ticket."

"I got you a ticket."

"You got a ticket for me?"

"Yes, I got a ticket for you. Get dressed."

I got dressed and in no time at all I was sitting a table watching important Congress members, powerful news reporters, legends, athletes, and celebrities walk by with their dates. It was incredible. I was just happy to be there. Imagine my surprise when the mistress of ceremonies began to speak about "a young man from Hope, Arkansas" and the Presidency. *I know they're not going to bring the President out here.* I couldn't believe it when President Clinton walked on stage. I had always wanted to hear President Clinton speak. The whole evening was incredible. Here I was Valerie Rose from Minnesota listening to President Clinton deliver a speech to a banquet hall where I was seated only a few feet away from him.

An hour before, I had no ticket, no prospect for a ticket, and no Washington contacts. I'm telling you, if you call on it, the Spirit can work all kind of magic. I'm not exactly sure of how it all happened, but what I do know is that before I set out on this mission, I spoke my truth into the Universe, "I thank you God for what you have already done." I also know that because I made that one simple statement, I was experienced a night that I will remember and cherish for the rest of my life. I just wish that while I was lying in bed, wallowing in self-pity, that I had remained steadfast in my refusal to doubt and taken my shower before the call instead of afterwards.

After awhile, when you learn to release all doubt, you stop wondering *if* it will happen and begin to wonder when and how it will be manifested. I had never been to Washington, D.C. I was in awe of being in the presence of all of those people that I was only used to seeing as images moving across the television screen. But because I had the opportunity to see some of them in a social setting, I made an important discovery: even though these people are very powerful, affluent, and influential, when it all comes down to it, they are just people. They are just people and President Clinton is just a man. Granted, he is one of the most powerful men on the planet, but he is still just a man. We are so accustomed to seeing these people as images moving across a television screen that, in a way, that's what they become... a conceptual image. But the reality is that they are human beings, just like you and me.

Recognize that we all have the power.

> # RECOGNIZE
> the opportunity.

RECOGNIZE
opportunity when it presents itself.

On opportunity:

> "Opportunity is missed by most people because it is
> dressed in overalls and looks like work."
> – Thomas Alva Edison

> "A pessimist sees the difficulty in every opportunity;
> an optimist sees the opportunity in every difficulty."
> – Sir Winston Churchill (1874-1965)

"The Missed Opportunity"

I was traveling alone with my two daughters, ages 1 and 8 at
the time. We were going to Memphis with a connecting
flight in Cincinnati. I'd promised to share my hotel room
with my sister, Helayna (not her real name), who had already
arrived in Memphis.

Before I continue, I should point out that air travel with a
baby can prove to be somewhat of a challenge, but air travel
alone, with a one-year old, a car seat, another child and
luggage, can truly test one's faith. But, somehow I'd
managed to do it. My bags were checked, my children and
I were comfortably strapped in, and I was ready for the
second leg of our trip when the flight attendant made an

announcement over the intercom. Apparently, they had overbooked the flight and were offering $1,000 in flight vouchers, plus hotel room and dinner vouchers for the evening to any passengers that were willing to give up their seats and spend the night in Cincinnati. I did not raise my hand. I considered it briefly, but I was alone and traveling with the children and a load of luggage. I was not eager to step out of my comfort zone and take on that challenge. Besides, I reasoned, Helayna was waiting for us.

I sat there. They made the announcement a few more times and then the flight attendant said, "We need *three* more people." The Universe can be very direct at times.

I continued to sit there with my two girls, reasoning, in part, that Helayna was waiting for us. When I arrived in Memphis, I woke up and realized my mistake, but it was too late. If I had been paying attention, the three of us could have enjoyed the cordial hospitality of Cincinnati for one night. And to this day, I could have been enjoying and reaping the benefits of the $3,000 in flight vouchers. Never mind the intelligence factor, it was a missed opportunity. I was not paying attention.

Pay attention. Be aware. Be open to the prospect of something higher. Be open to the possibility that something else is going on... something higher. When the Universe offers you an opportunity, you have to be in tune with it. You have to be ready. Sometimes life gives us opportunities that we should take. Trust your instincts, they are usually right.

Recognize that another word for opportunity is chance.
Take a chance on you.

RECOGNIZE

that failure is just a tool for your
eventual success.

On failure:

"The highway to success." – John Keats

"Not the falling down, but the staying down."
– Mary Pickford

"In the middle of difficulty lies opportunity."
– Albert Einstein

"Many people dream of success. To me, success can
only be achieved through repeated failure and
introspection." – Soichiro Honda, founder of Honda Motors

"Every wall is a door." – Emerson

On success:

"Success isn't measured by the position you reach in
life, it's measured by the obstacles you overcome."
– Booker T. Washington

"The Rejection"

Failure is just a learning tool for success. When I submitted
the manuscript for my first novel, *Cappuccino in the Winter*, to
the publishing house that I was targeting, it was rejected. I
was crushed. Among a few other things, the editor said the
pacing in the front of the book was too slow. Pacing? I had
no idea what she was talking about. This prompted me to go

to the bookstore to find some books on the subject. I picked up some books about pacing and some other reference books about story structure. After devouring these books, I went back and read what I had written in the front of the book. Instantly, I recognized the problem. Because of my studies, it became clear to me what I had done and what I had not done. I rewrote the front of the book and prepared to resubmit the manuscript to the publishing house. What this "failure" did was open my mind to something that I did not yet understand, which then prompted me to get more information. I studied more on the subject, did some rewrites, and, in the process, learned a lot about building a solid story. Ultimately, that "failure" not only helped me to create a better book, but it gave me the opportunity to build my skills as a writer, as well.

Nearing the end of my rewrite, another publisher emailed me to tell me that they would like to publish my book. They indicated that they really liked the book, but that they would like for me to work on the pacing in the front of the book. Because of my previous "failure," I had already worked on improving the pacing of the book and was very close to completion. What I perceived to be a "failure", turned out to be learning tool for my eventual success with *Cappuccino in the Winter*.

It's all in the way that you look at it. If you perceive that you have failed and you let it stop you, then you have failed. But, if you don't let that stop you, then it won't. Learn from your "failure" and try it again, employing what you've learned from the last time. Eventually, you will be successful.

Recognize the opportunity in "failure".

RECOGNIZE

that adversity may be working for our
higher good.

On adversity:

> "If I had a formula for bypassing trouble, I would
> not pass it round. Trouble creates a capacity to
> handle it. I don't embrace trouble; that's as bad as
> treating it as an enemy. But I do say meet it as a
> friend, for you'll see a lot of it and had better be on
> speaking terms with it." – Oliver Wendell Holmes

> "Adversity causes some men to break; others to
> break records." – William A. Ward

> "Adversity is like a strong wind. It tears away from us
> all but the things that cannot be torn, so that we see
> ourselves as we really are." – Arthur Golden

"The SUV"

A few years back, a Japanese company came out with an SUV
that was sort of a hybrid between a car and a sports utility
vehicle. I bought one—big mistake. One day, as I was pulling
into a parking spot, the car revved by itself and began to
accelerate. Fortunately, I was able to step on the brakes
quickly enough to avoid hitting the cement pole next to me
or the car in front of me. I shifted the vehicle into park,
turned off the engine, and got out.

I called the car dealership and told them that the car had a spontaneous acceleration problem. I told them to come get the car; I refused to drive it. I also asked for a refund. Neither the company nor the dealership was receptive to this. When I reported it to the appropriate authorities, I found that there were many other people like me who had run into this same problem with vehicles built by this particular automaker. Even though both the dealership and the company itself were aware of these complaints, they wouldn't acknowledge that there was a problem. To make a long story short, I lost $7,000 on the deal. While going through it was painful, in hindsight, I realize that it was better to have lost $7,000 than to have caused someone to lose a life. There are two things to take away from this story:

- I simply was not meant to have that vehicle. I have since read tragic stories on the National Highway Traffic and Safety's website and other websites about people who have ended up killing people because of the spontaneous acceleration problem in this and other vehicles made by that automaker. While I lost out monetarily, I understand that money is replaceable. It's important to understand that something else was going on. Taking a life because I was driving that vehicle was something that at the core of my being, I was not choosing to experience. It was not in the plan. Therefore, the loss of $7,000 was a small price to pay when viewed from a wider perspective. It's all in the way you look at it.

- One day, that Japanese company will pay the price for knowing about this problem, not doing anything about it, and continuing to sell the vehicle. I know this to be true, because what you do comes back to you. It may come in a different form, but it will come back.

RECOGNIZE

that if you choose to be happy, you will be happy.

On happiness:

"The best way to cheer yourself up is to cheer everybody else up." – Mark Twain

"Happiness is as a butterfly which, when pursued, is always beyond our grasp, but which if you will sit down quietly, may alight upon you."
– Nathaniel Hawthorne

"Happiness depends upon ourselves." – Aristotle

"To live happily is an inward power of the soul."
– Marcus Aurelius

"It is all within yourself, in your way of thinking."
– Marcus Aurelius

"The Kingdom of Heaven is within you… Seek ye first the Kingdom of Heaven and all things will be added unto you." – Jesus of Nazareth

You are the architect of your life. You and no one else. You always have a choice about how to be and respond. Life throws some crazy stuff at us sometimes, but accept it. Be at peace with it. Appreciate what you have and be happy anyway. People will be attracted to the light that you are shining.

"The Disgruntled Ticket Agent"

I was at an airport recently when an overworked ticket agent went off on my travel companion and me. At first when she started yelling, I think I might have said something like there's no need for you to raise your voice. But her response was to get even louder. My companion and I both then responded by screaming back at her and demanding her name.

I often think back on that moment. The impact that I could have had on this woman and on myself would have been much greater had I chosen a different response. And my karma would have been straight too. If I could go back to that moment, I would have closed my eyes and called on the peace from within, and completed the transaction while maintaining complete composure. If I had taken this approach, I wouldn't have been steamin' then and I wouldn't be sweatin' it now. I had the power to choose otherwise, but I didn't. I chose to engage into negativity right along with her.

This incident was one of many that we had with the airline. I ended up drafting a courteous complaint letter; however, I chose not to include the ticketing agent's name. I was consciously aware of the karma and negative vibes that would surely come back to me if I chose to continue with that cycle of negativity.

You are probably asking yourself how you can be happy when negative things are happening to you. The answer is, find something good in your life. There's always something good. Then focus in on that.

Recognize that happiness is a choice.

RECOGNIZE
that you're going to be all right.

"Beginnings"

Things do change. Don't think of change as the end of something wonderful; think of it as the beginning of something wonderful.

Recognize that you are going to be all right.

RECOGNIZE
that death is simply a change in form.

On death:

> "Death is not extinguishing the light; it is putting out the lamp because dawn has come".
> – Rabindranath Tagore

> "When the soul shall emerge from its sheath."
> – Marcus Aurelius

> "The undiscovered country." – William Shakespeare

> "Is death the last sleep? No – it is the last and final awakening." – Sir Walter Scott

> "Don't grieve. Anything you lose comes round in another form." – Rumi

"I look upon death to be as necessary to the constitution as sleep. We shall rise refreshed in the morning." – Benjamin Franklin

"Our birth is but a sleep and a forgetting; The Soul that rises with us, our life's Star, Hath had elsewhere its setting. And cometh from afar." – William Wordsworth

"You see that who you are isn't moving in time. Time is describing the incarnations, the packing changes." – Ram Dass

"Know, therefore, that from the greater silence I shall return... Forget not that I shall come back to you... A little while, a moment of rest upon the wind, and another woman shall bear me." – Kahlil Gibran

"Who says the eternal being does not exist? Who says the sun has gone out? Someone who climbs up on the roof and closes his eyes tight, and says, I don't see anything." – Jalalu'l-din Rumi

"It is the secret of the world that all things subsist and do not die, but only retire a little from sight and afterwards return again. Nothing is dead; men feign themselves dead, and endure mock funerals... and there they stand looking out of the window, sound and well, in some strange new disguise." —Ralph Waldo Emerson

"It is no more surprising to be born once than to be born twice: everything in nature is resurrection." – Francois Voltaire

"It is a strong proof of men knowing most things before birth, that when mere children they grasp innumerable facts with such speed as to show that they are not then taking them in for the first time, but are remembering and recalling them."
– Marcus Tullius Cicero

"I hold that when a person dies, his Soul returns again to earth; Arrayed in some new flesh-disguise, another mother gives him birth. With sturdier limbs and brighter brain, the old Soul takes the road again." – John Masefield

"Everything science has taught me strengthens my belief in the continuity of our spiritual existence after death. I believe in an immortal soul. Science has proved that nothing disintegrates into nothingness. Life and soul, therefore, cannot disintegrate into nothingness, and so are immortal."
– Werner von Braun

"The soul is immortal – well then, if I shall always live, I must have lived before, lived for a whole eternity." – Leo Tolstoy

"The tomb is not a blind alley: it is a thoroughfare. It closes on the twilight. It opens on the dawn."
– Victor Hugo

"The soul of man is like to water; from Heaven it cometh, to Heaven it riseth… And then returning to earth, forever alternating." – Johann Wolfgang von Goethe

"My life often seemed to me like a story that has no beginning and no end. I had the feeling that I was

an historical fragment, an excerpt for which the
preceding and succeeding text was missing. I could
well imagine that I might have lived in former
centuries and there encountered questions I was not
yet able to answer; that I had been born again
because I had not fulfilled the task given to me."
– Carl Jung

"Sunrise. Sunset. Sunrise."

Do you really think that your loved one's spirit is gone? Do
you really think that when your loved one passed away that
they ceased to exist? If you really think about it, you will
understand that his or her spirit transcends earthly form.
Just because you can't see him or her, it doesn't mean that
they're not there. Consider the potency of their essence.
Isn't it too strong to just disappear completely?

You must understand that they are with you every day. All
day. Maybe you can't see them, but they are there with you,
supporting you, and directing you. Sometimes if you pay
close attention, they will let you know that they are there.
This may be a feeling, a thought, or even a dream. It may
even come in the form of words that come directly out of
the mouth of someone you know. But whichever form the
contact takes, you'll know from whom it comes.

Consider also the possibility that they are even closer than
you imagine. Have you ever watched a candle burn out?
When a candle is put out, it doesn't mean that it can't be lit
up again. It doesn't mean that a very real physical flame that
can and will burn your finger will not manifest again.
Perhaps your loved one is closer than you think, but in a
form that you won't necessarily recognize. Is the idea of
reincarnation so improbable? Can you really, beyond a

shadow of a doubt, know that this does not occur? At any rate, even if you don't believe in it, it's something to ponder.

Recognize that the flame that burns within never dies; it is eternal.

RECOGNIZE
   that adversity is many times
   Nature's way of giving us a prompt.

On adversity:

> "In the middle of difficulty lies opportunity."
> – Albert Einstein

> "When written in Chinese, the word crisis is composed of two characters. One represents danger, and the other represents opportunity."
> – John F. Kennedy

> "In the depth of winter, I finally learned that there was in me an invincible summer." – Albert Camus

> "Every wall is a door." – Emerson

"Your True Colors"

It's been said that inside adversity is opportunity. It is not uncommon for the world to tell you no. Perhaps, even that is its job.

To push you forward to motivate you to discover your true potential. Recognize that if something that you would consider as bad, is going on in your life, it could be that it's a point of healing... and ultimately, something good is probably going to come from it. Consider the possibility that adversity is your opportunity to rise to the occasion.

"Wilma"

As a child, Wilma Rudolph was plagued with many serious illnesses, including double pneumonia, scarlet fever, and polio. Polio is a crippling disease that deformed her left leg and foot. The doctors said Wilma would never walk again. But twice a week Wilma's mother would take her to a hospital fifty miles away. Eventually, with physical therapy, Wilma was able to walk again, with use of metal leg brace. By age 12, she could walk normally. Wilma started playing basketball with her brothers. She went on to win three gold medals at the 1960 Olympics in Rome, Italy and was named "The World's Fastest Woman."

"Scott"

Scott Hamilton was also plagued by childhood illness. At age five he simply stopped growing, his body was not absorbing the vitamins and nutrients it needed to grow. There was no known cure for Scott's illness, because the doctor's didn't even know what it was. As a result, Scott was sickly and constantly in the hospital. By age nine, he decided to take up skating. Amazingly, when he began to skate, his health improved dramatically. Scott went on to become a US and Olympic figure skating champion.

Life can push hard on us sometimes. But, that's life. When life gets tough, you can either lie down and surrender or you can take charge. How do you take charge?

- Educate yourself.
- Spend time alone to connect with your spirit.
- Decide what you are going to do about what's happened.
- Take some positive action.
- Never give up.
- Turn inward for strength and then rise to the occasion.

Recognize that you are invincible.

RECOGNIZE

that pain means growth.

On pain:

"I saw sorrow turning to clarity." – Yoko Ono

"Spiritual Growth Spurts"

What is it that you're going through? What you think is a terrible ending, may in fact, be a fresh, new beginning. You just can't see it yet. Trust that the Universe is working for you and not against you. Consider the possibility that there's a higher purpose to what you're going through. My Daddy always says, "Trouble don't last always." I believe that to be true. Trust that it will get better. The Universe may be prompting you –nudging you—to be on your way to a new and better you.

So, if you are at your lowest point, just know that it will get better. Life is a rhythm, racing from one extreme to the next. Recognize that you're gonna be okay. It will get better.

Recognize, my friend, that it will get better.

RECOGNIZE

that worry is not constructive.

On worry:

> "How much have cost us the evils that
> never happened!" – Thomas Jefferson

> "Do not anticipate trouble, or worry about what may
> never happen. Keep in the sunlight."
> – Benjamin Franklin

> "Never trouble trouble till trouble troubles you."
> – Unknown

> "It ain't no use putting up your umbrella till it rains."
> – Alice Caldwell Rice

"The Computer-Based Training"

Two teammates and I were working on a project to develop some computer-based training. We broke the project into three sections. After we had finished development, we piloted the sections to the users. Before the pilot class, I put in a quick change. I didn't test it, because the change was so small that it didn't seem necessary. The organizational structure of the pilot class was such that each developer observed the users as they ran through the pilot for someone else's work. The users were giving constructive criticism on everyone's work. But, when I overheard them commenting on my work, I thought that the comments were resulting from the quick change that I'd put in without testing.

I had spent the entire weekend worrying that my training was not working correctly. I was also upset because I thought the users did not see what I had spent weeks working on. Instead, I thought they'd seen the result of something that took only a half-hour to do. It turns out my training was working properly. The users were just commenting on some constructive changes in the content. But my whole weekend was ruined worrying that my training was not working correctly. What a waste of time!

Recognize that worry is not productive use of your time and energy.

RECOGNIZE
your purpose.

RECOGNIZE
that persistence has big payoffs.

On persistence:

"Obstacles are those frightful things you see when you take your eyes off your goals." – unknown

"Our greatest glory is not in never failing, but in rising up every time we fail." – Ralph Waldo Emerson

"It is not because things are difficult that we do not dare, it is because we do not dare that they are difficult." – Seneca

"The heights by great men reached and kept were not obtained by sudden flight. But they, while their companions slept, were toiling upward in the night." – Thomas S. Monson

"If the going is real easy, beware, you may be headed down hill." – unknown

"Never, never, never give up." – Winston Churchill

On success:

"The reward of toil." – Sophocles

Many times the world will tell you that you can't. Perhaps, even, that is its job. Your job is to tap into your light and defy the world by proving it wrong. Your job is to prove that you can.

These days you can find a range of different shows on TV that feature celebrity profiles and their roads to success. I don't watch a lot of TV. But when I do, I tend to watch these biographies. What's interesting about all of these stories is that while the celebrities they profile run the gamut from presidents to screen legends to powerful news personalities to rap stars, they all have one common thread: the language of success.

The Language of Success:
- "She was determined..."
- "He always knew he was going to be..."
- "But he never gave up."
- "She persevered."
- "He wouldn't give up..."
- "Everybody said I was crazy... everybody said I couldn't do it."
- "...But she refused to take no for an answer..."

But, successful people don't have to be movie stars or presidents. Have you ever been around someone who was determined to make it? People like this often speak with bold confidence, refusing to accept the possibility that they may not succeed. They know, without a doubt, that they will succeed.

Universal Law

"Didn't I just talk to you? I told you no [idiot]."

Never give up.

My nephew is stationed at a military base near Venice, Italy. I decided to visit him. I didn't concern myself with money. I just decided to visit. In January, I called the airline to make arrangements to visit him in June. Again and again, I was told no, as *I was trying to use a frequent flyer ticket and availability to such passengers was virtually non-existent due to black out dates*. Adding to the availability issue was the fact that summer is peak travel time for touring Europe. There was simply nothing available. But, I was relentless and kept calling. I was going to Italy. I had already made that determination. Once when I called back, the ticket agent said something like, "Didn't I just talk to you? I told you no [idiot]." Well, she didn't say idiot, but I know that's what she meant. But, I didn't care. I kept calling.

Sometimes I was even chastised, with comments like, "People generally make these arrangements a year in advance [idiot]." Well, she didn't say idiot, but I know that's what she meant. But, I didn't care. I kept calling. I was trying to go through anywhere—Miami, Amsterdam, London. I figured that once I got across the water, I could just catch a train or something. Again and again, I was told there was no availability. Once I called and they said that they could get me over there, but they could not get me back. Obviously, that was not an option. Still I persisted. I was determined. One night after I'd put my children to bed, I decided to call again. The ticket agent again told me that there was no availability. Then out of the blue, she said, "You know... have you considered flying into Milan? There's an Italian airline

that is a sister to ours and..."
I just laughed. "Great," I said, "book it." And I was on my way
to Milan.

When I got home from Italy, I received four unexpected
checks. Two were from the government (the tax rebates),
the other two were from a different source. Think I didn't
take 'em to the bank?

It's 2:30 AM as I type this. Don't give up on your dream.
Never give up. Keep at it. Be resolute.

Recognize that success is earned through persistence.

RECOGNIZE
that negativity competes with and depletes positivity.

On negativity:

> "People deal too much with the negative, with what
> is wrong. Why not try and see positive things, to just
> touch those things and make them bloom?"
> – Thich Nhat Hanh

> "I will not let anyone walk through my mind with
> their dirty feet!" – Mahatma Gandhi

"On the Positive Tip"

Negativity. Move away from it—move toward positivity. You
can choose how to expend your energy. Recognize that if

you choose to engage in negativity, as soon as you do, your attention has turned away from positivity. It's difficult to create something positive if you're focused on the negative. Many I times must remind myself of this—it's an on-going process of consciousness and awareness. Ultimately, the choice is yours, but understand that the choice that you make has consequences.

If, for example, you are over there gossiping with Laquisha about what Eboni and Akeem over there were doing yesterday or contemplating what lie you are going to tell your other girlfriend when she comes to confront you (and you know she will) or just plain scheming, then you are robbing your mind of the opportunity to create and develop a new idea. You're wasting time. You could be using that energy for something positive. Speaking of using your energy positively, be careful about how much TV you watch. The message here is not to yank your television out of the wall and throw it out the window. But you might do well to cut back on some of those hours in front of the set, particular time spent watching the news. A lot of that stuff rolling across your TV can be a real downer. It's good to be informed, but you have to monitor what's being fed into your consciousness. Understand that when negativity is being fed into your consciousness, your consciousness is busy. More than likely, it will be too busy to create anything positive. Besides, when something really important happens, people will let you know.

If someone else is not helping you believe in yourself, you need to ask yourself why and figure out what—if anything— you're going to do about it. You have to make a decision. You have a choice. People can give you advice and suggestions on what to do, but no one can tell you what is right for you, but you. What is your inner voice telling you?

Recognize that using your energy wisely is the best thing you can do for yourself. Don't waste it by saying negative things. Recognize that if you are trying to stay focused on the positive, it only makes sense to surround your self with positive things and positive people.

Recognize that you have a choice.

RECOGNIZE

that tomorrow is not promised to anyone.

On today:

"Yesterday is history. Tomorrow is a mystery.
And today? Today is a gift. That's why we call it
The Present." – Babatunde Olatunji

"Yesterday is ashes; tomorrow wood. Only today does
the fire burn brightly." – Old Eskimo saying

"Somebody should tell us, right at the start of our
lives, that we are dying. Then we might live life to
the limit, every minute of every day. Do it! I say.
Whatever you want to do, do it now. There are only
so many tomorrows." – Michael Landon

"Be here now." – Baba Ram Das

"The place to be happy is here, the time to be happy
is now." – Robert Ingersoll

"Seize the moment. Remember all those women on the Titanic who waved off the dessert cart."
– Erma Bombeck, American Humorist

"Begin doing what you want to do now. We are not living in eternity. We have only this moment, sparkling like a star in our hand and melting like a snowflake." – Marie Beyon Ray

"Why not seize the pleasure at once? How often is happiness destroyed by preparation? Foolish preparation?" – Jane Austen

"Do It Now."

Do it now. Take some action. Get the ball rolling. If you don't, who will? It's your dream. No one else will make your dream happen. Your life is now. Stop talking about tomorrow. Do it now, whatever it is. Take that trip! Finish that manuscript. Write that song. Get that degree. Develop that business plan. Whatever it is, take some action toward your dream. A small action is better than no action at all. Be creative and thank the Universe for giving you direction. You are an extraordinary and creative being.

Recognize... that life is a wild, perplexing ride. Notice it! Enjoy it! Don't let it pass you by.

RECOGNIZE

that action is the first step to your
eventual success.

On success:

"Not the result of spontaneous combustion.
You must set yourself on fire." – Reginald Leach

On action:

"Well done is better than well said." – Ben Franklin

"Deeds are better than words are. Actions mightier
than boastings." – Henry Wadsworth Longfellow

"Action may not always bring happiness; but there is
no happiness without action." – Benjamin Disraeli

"Shoot for the moon. Even if you miss it you will
land among the stars." – Les Brown

I am reminded of a joke someone told once me.

"The Lottery Ticket"

Mary lost her job. Fraught with worry, that night she got
down on her knees and prayed. "God, please, please, let me
win the lottery."
The next day the lottery came and went, but Mary was not a
winner. Because she'd lost her job, Mary was unable to pay
the payments on her car so it was repossessed.
Again, Mary went home, got on her knees, and prayed

earnestly. "God, please. I don't know what I'm going to do. Please, please let me win the lottery."

The next day the lottery came and went, but Mary was not a winner. Mary was getting deeper and deeper into debt. With no income, and no prospects, Mary could do nothing when they foreclosed on her home.

In the pouring rain, her children looked on as Mary again fell to her knees in front of a park bench to pray. "God, please. I'm begging you. I have no where to take my children. God, please, I'm asking you. I'm begging you, please let me win the lottery."

The next day the lottery came and went, but Mary was not a winner. Soon after, child welfare services discovered that she and her children were living in the streets. They accused Mary of being an unfit mother and began proceedings to take her children away.

Despondent and angry, Mary took a walk in the park so that she could talk to God alone. "I don't understand this," she said. You are supposed to be a benevolent, kind, loving God – A God who hears and answers all prayers. I have been praying to you earnestly in faith that you would answer my prayer, but you refuse to answer."

Suddenly, she heard a loud crack in the sky and then a loud booming voice. "Dang, Mary, meet me half way. Buy a ticket!!!"

This anecdote is not meant to endorse the lottery. The point I am trying to make here is for you to *take some action.* Nothing will happen unless and until you take some action.

When you do, as long as it's in your best interest, the
Universe will support you.

*Recognize that the Universe is waiting for you to make up
your mind so that it can respond appropriately.*

RECOGNIZE
that you are the key to your dreams.

On dreams:

> "**Now** is the operative word. Everything you put in
> your way is just a method of putting off the hour
> when you could actually be doing your dream. You
> don't need endless time and perfect conditions. Do
> it now. Do it today. Do it for twenty minutes and
> watch your heart start beating." – Barbara Sher

> "I have learned this at least by my experiment: if
> one advances confidently in the direction of his
> dreams, and endeavors to live the life he has
> imagined, he will meet with a success unexpected
> in common hours." – Henry David Thoreau

> "You eat in dreams, the custard of the day."
> – Alexander Pope

"Dream Your Dream."

You are the architect of your own life. Give your mind the opportunity to be silent and then dream your dream. Yes, dream your dream, but, be about doing something about it, too. And don't even let it occur in your mind that you can't do it. Eliminate the possibility that anything else can happen. Think big.

> Dream your dream.
> Believe your dream.
> Live your dream!

You are the impetus. You are the key. No one else will put forth the effort to make your dream happen. Sure, they may help you along, once you get started. But, they won't do it for you. You are responsible for making that choice – making that decision. You are the driving force, the catalyst, the spark.

Recognize that you are the key to opening your door.

RECOGNIZE
that you are a creative force in the Universe.

On creativity:

> "You have only one source of creativity – your own unique talents, skills, perspectives, and experiences. You can't be creative with someone else's stuff, because creativity, by definition, is the process of translating who you are into some outward

manifestation. It doesn't matter whether that is a painting, an ad campaign, a holiday dinner, a business report, or the raising of a healthy child. The creative process can be applied to all of our activities, eventually yielding a truly creative life."
– G. Lynne Snead and Joyce Wycoff

"Discontent translated into art." – Eric Hoffer

"Make visible what, without you, might perhaps never been seen." – Robert Bresson

How many times have you looked at someone else's work, creation, or success and said to yourself, "Well, golly gee… I could've done that." Well… maybe you didn't say golly gee… But my question to you is: *Why didn't you? Or more to the point, Why don't you? What's stopping you? Why do you keep bringing up all of these excuses why you can't do something?* Take some time to ask yourself that question and come up with an answer. When you do, you need to make the determination of what's good for you and is it worth it.

Recognize that creativity is therapeutic.

RECOGNIZE
that your Creator created you to create.

On the Creator:

"Every human is an artist. The dream of your life is to make beautiful art." – don Miguel Ruiz

"Life isn't about finding yourself. Life is about creating yourself." – George Bernard Shaw

And just exactly what is it you are supposed to be creating? Only you can answer that question. And unless you quiet the noise and spend some time alone to figure it out, how will you know?

Recognize that you are a creative force in the universe.

Life

The journey...

LOVE-HATE • PEACE-WAR • FAST-SLOW
PHYSICAL-SPIRITUAL • JOY-PAIN • UP-DOWN
HERE-THERE • STOP-GO • GOOD-EVIL
LIGHT-DARK • RICH-POOR • BLACK-WHITE
MAN-WOMAN • BOY-GIRL • CRAZY-SANE
SWEET-BITTER • HAPPY-SAD • RIGHT-LEFT
CONSTANT-CHANGE • ILLUSION-REALITY
ONE-MANY • AWAKE-ASLEEP • DIFFERENT-SAME

Of life...

Existence
Energy
Spirit
Being
Reality
Permanence
Consciousness
Zest
Vivacity
The Human Condition
A Grand Illusion
A Deep Sleep
A Dream
A Spiritual Journey

RECOGNIZE
the splendor of Creation.

On Creation:

> "The mystical is not how the world is, but that it is."
> – Ludwig Wittgenstein

> "Every tree and plant in the meadow seemed to be dancing, those which average eyes would see as fixed and still." – Rumi

> "There are only two ways to live your life. One is as though nothing is a miracle. The other is as if everything is a miracle." – Albert Einstein

> "Earth's crammed with Heaven."
> – Elizabeth Barrett Browning

> "To be alive, to be able to see, to walk… it's all a miracle. I have adopted the technique of living life from miracle to miracle." – Arthur Rubinstein

Creation is a true wonder. We lay witness to the most amazing phenomenon; yet, we don't pay attention to it. We act as though it is a mundane, trivial event. It's like the world's best magician is forever performing the most exotic, extraordinary illusions and we simply refuse to applaud. The leaves on the trees change colors before our eyes. It's nothing short of magic. But, we act as though it's nothing. We watch, but we don't pay attention.

Creation is a true wonder. Notice it! Appreciate it! The next time it snows, stop, look and appreciate the notion that every single snowflake is inexplicably different. Appreciate Nature's display of its awesome beauty. Have you ever witnessed a sunset that was so stunning that you could hardly breathe? In the evening when the sun goes down, stop and watch it make its way. Appreciate its beauty. Then watch the stars magically appear in the black blanket of night. It's an awesome spectacle, when you really think about it. The next time you pass by a rose bush, stop to smell the roses.

Have you ever stopped and watched a Swallowtail butterfly's carefree float through a field of wildflowers? Or watched a dragonfly soar into the sun? Or watched a tiny ant carry a crumb of bread through a grassy road? Have you ever stopped to listen to crickets at night? Have you ever inhaled deeply after a summer rain or a brisk, winter snow?

Have you ever marveled at the stretch marks in the trunk of a 100-year-old tree? Take time out to really notice your surroundings. It could be the intricacy of a leaf on a tree, or the intense almost blinding yellow of a simple dandelion.

We share the planet with some amazing creatures... some exotic and some not so exotic. Ever watched a fly up close? I know they can be pesky little things, but if you really look closely, they are actually kind of fascinating, with their tiny webbed wings and busy little legs. Their eyes are almost bigger than they are. Can you imagine the creative intelligence that had to go into the engineering of such a creature? And the rest of the creatures on this planet?

The next time you touch your child's hand, take some time to marvel at its tinyness. Then give thanks for it. Take the time. Pay attention and soon you will be filled with wonder and amazement. We share the planet with some amazing creatures.

Have you ever seen your child's eyes sparkle with joy from across the room as she played in the water on a warm sunny afternoon without a care in the world? Try it sometime, it will bring you joy. Be in awe of it. Be inspired by it. Let it move you. Let it inspire you. Have you ever felt the love that is present in the room when you read your child a simple bed time story? Have you ever watched your child's amusement explode from a smile into a jubilant, unbridled belly laugh?

Be thankful. Be aware and pay attention.

Have you ever stood still in a park and watched sunrays skip through the leaves of trees or listened to the breeze as it flows through them? Or listened to the crickets sing? Or felt the brilliance of the sun on your face without stressing about UV-Protection.

Every fall, millions of Monarch butterflies migrate south to the Mountain Sanctuaries in Mexico. Tourists come to witness this incredible phenomenon—they describe the trees, air, mountainsides, and forest floor as being covered in red and black flutters.

Nature is wondrous. This is one example of Nature's many phenomena. Take the time to absorb the magnificence of it all.

"Mommy, why you looking at me?"

I have two daughters, 11 and 3. Both are beautiful. Both seemingly wise beyond their years. Sometimes they catch me staring at them.

"Mommy, why you looking at me?" They ask.

"Because you're beautiful," I respond quickly, looking away. But my true response is a lot deeper than I let on. When one of them catches me, and then asks this very simple question, inside I'm really thinking that I can't believe that I helped create these stunningly beautiful miracles. I say miracles, because first there was nothing, then suddenly, from nowhere, there were these living, breathing, moving things, that I helped to create. These living, breathing moving things, just materialized out of nothing – really when you sit down and think about it. These things with these wide eyes and tiny little fingers, these beautiful chocolate jewels. I wonder, where did they come from? Sometimes I ask them. "Where you come from?"

"From daycare," says the littlest one.

"Where you come from?" I say again.

"From you, Mommy," says the older one.

It was 3:00 in the morning when I decided to stop work and chomp on some microwave popcorn before going to bed. So, I slid into bed and started reading a magazine. Not long after, the little one comes into my room, rubbing her eyes.

"It's sleepy time; you're supposed to be in bed," I say.

"Popcorn," she says and joyfully, jumps into my bed.

Again, I stare at her in awe, watching as her tiny teeth gobble down the kernels.

"Mommy, why are you looking at me?"

"Because you're beautiful."

"Oh."

"You know you're beautiful, right?"

"Mm. Hm.," she says.

"Where you come from?"

"From you, Mommy," she says "from you."

"Oh."

I'm telling you, man, that's joy!

Recognize the awe-inspiring beauty when you see it.

RECOGNIZE

that if you are afraid to live your
life, you will be afraid to *live* your life.

On living:

"Every man dies. Not every man really lives."
– William Wallace (From the movie *Braveheart*)

"If you had the choice between killing yourself and
doing the thing that you're really afraid of, why not
do the thing that you're really afraid of?"
– paraphrased, Tom Hanks in the movie *Joe Vs. the Volcano*

"Live! Yes! Life is a banquet and most suckers are
starving to death." – Patrick Dennis, "Auntie Mame"

"There is no goal better than this one: to know as
you lie on your deathbed that you lived your true
life, and you did whatever made you happy."
– Steve Chandler, "100 Ways to Motivate Yourself"

Ancient Egyptians believed that upon death they
would be asked two questions and their answers
would determine whether they could continue their
journey in the afterlife. The first question was, "Did
you bring joy?" The second was, "Did you find joy?"
– Leo Buscaglia

"Anything I've ever done that ultimately was
worthwhile… initially scared me to death."
– Betty Bender

On fear:

> "Avoiding danger is no safer in the long run than outright exposure. Life is either a daring adventure or nothing." – Helen Keller

If you want to go on an exotic vacation and your husband or your wife or your friends don't want to go, go by yourself. Experience life. The universe will support you.

"The Hook-Up at the Principale di Savoia "

I decided to go to Italy. I didn't worry about the money because I knew the Universe would support me. So, I threw caution to the wind and made the arrangements. Before I left for my trip, I'd read an article in *Essence* magazine that was on the subject of Milan, one of my soon to be destinations. The article described the Principale di Savoia as the most expensive hotel in Milan.

My niece, Starlette, was my traveling companion. Our itinerary was to take us from JFK to Milan, Venice, Luzerne (Switzerland), the Italian Lakes District, back to Venice and back to Milan and then back to the States.

We were in Venice when Starlette decided that she liked Milan better than Venice. We decided to change our itinerary to skip our return trip to Venice, so that we could instead return to Milan. I was in a phone booth in the lobby of our hotel in Venice, about to rearrange our plans, when I jokingly said to Starlette that we should stay at the Principale di Savoia. "Yes," she said, "we should." I was half joking, but she was serious. I thought, *When will I ever be in Italy again? Go for it!* So, we turned to the hotel clerk, told him to cancel our reservation for our return, and to make reservations at the Principale di Savoia. "But that hotel charges $400 a night," he said. My niece and I looked at each other and smiled, "Yes, we know."

We were in Lake Gardo in Northern Italy when it was nearing time to return to Milan. We had planned to return by train, but we said what the heck. *When will we ever be in Italy again?* So we rented a limo to drive us. We arrived at the hotel and was greeted by the doorman who opened our door and helped us out of the car.

The Principale di Savoia gave us a very nice suite, with full view of the front courtyard, but there was one problem: the bathtub was dirty. Or so we thought. Turns out it was stained. But, when you're paying that kind of money, you want only the best right? We requested a new room. Unfortunately, the only rooms that were available were not as big and not as nice as the one we had, so we stayed the night in the room that we had.

The next day, as I was enjoying a European massage, my niece saw the hotel manager who had tried to help us the night before. Starlette explained the reasons why we decided to just stay in the room that we had and asked if there were any rooms available now. So when my massage was over, my niece was waiting for me. She had a big smile on her face. "C'mon Val, let's go back to the room." You have to understand that service is of the utmost importance at the Principale di Savoia. Girlfriend had hooked us up in an "Elegant" suite, that lived up to its namesake. Marble walls, chandeliers, and that was just the beginning. The Principale di Savoia takes the notion of service, very, very seriously. As such, management took money off the bill and for about $200 a night, we ended up staying in an "Elegant" suite at the most luxurious hotel in Milan.

Rent *Joe vs. the Volcano*, with Tom Hanks and Meg Ryan. It speaks well to this subject.

Recognize that life is meant to be lived. So, live a little.

RECOGNIZE
that life is a dream experience, an illusion.

On the dream of life:

> "Your vision will become clear only when you look into your heart... Who looks outside, dreams. Who looks inside, awakens." – Carl Jung

> "We sometimes congratulate ourselves at the moment of waking from a troubled dream... it may be so at the moment of death." – Nathaniel Hawthorne

We come from a powerful energy source, and our purpose is to experience life and create life, all of it... The good and the bad. Life is full of opposites: left, right; up, down; black, white; summer, winter; joy, pain; good and bad. If you haven't experienced winter, it's difficult to fully appreciate summer. If you haven't experienced pain, how can you truly know joy? And if you've never experienced bad, how can you know, really know, good?

Recognize that when you are tired of dreaming, you can turn within.

RECOGNIZE
that life is love.

On love:

"Our highest word, and synonym for God."
– Ralph Waldo Emerson

"Spiritual Fire" – Emanuel Swendenborg

"Friendship set on fire." – Jeremy Taylor

"Love is life and if you miss love, you miss life."
– Leo Buscaglia

"Love is what's in the room with you at the holidays
if you stop opening presents and listen."
– Bobby, age 5

"If you want to learn to love better, you should start
with a friend who you hate." – Nikka, age 6

"I have died many a death in love, and yet, had I not
loved I would never have lived at all." – David Lasater

If you've ever been in love before, you know what an
incredible feeling it can be. If you're in love now – relish it,
pleasure in it, appreciate it, but mostly don't take it for
granted. Love your kids. Appreciate and listen to your elders.

Recognize that life is a wild, perplexing ride. Notice it!
Enjoy it! Don't let it pass you by.

RECOGNIZE

that not everyone is going to like you.

Recognize that not everyone will like what you have to say.
Not everyone is going to like you. But, so what? As long as
you remain focused on you and your inner growth, you will
be okay. The Universe will support you in your efforts.

You can't please everyone, so stop trying. Just be yourself.
Your job is to be kind and decent in how you respond to
people and to recognize and honor their light. If you do
that, you will be okay.

Recognize... that you're going to be all right.
Things do change.

RECOGNIZE

that appreciation brings you peace.

On appreciation:

> "Once we discover how to appreciate the timeless
> values in our daily experiences, we can enjoy the
> best things in life." – Harry Hepner

> "Prosperity depends more on wanting what you have
> than having what you want." – Geoffrey F. Abert

> "The foolish man seeks happiness in the distance,

the wise grows it under his feet." – James Oppenheim

On peace:

"Liberty in tranquility." – Cicero

The mere fact that you are reading this book and had the discretionary funds to purchase it is a blessing. Even if someone gave it to you, that, too, is a blessing.

When the weather produces freezing temperatures, rain, sleet, or snow, do you have a place to go to for shelter? Do you have enough to eat? Ask yourself these questions before you complain about how bad your life is. Stop stressing on what you don't have—focus on and appreciate what you do have.

If you have children, kiss their stubby little toes. Make up a bedtime story that features them and you as the main characters.

Recognize that there is peace within.

RECOGNIZE
that there's a magic formula
inside of you and it's called fear.

When you face your fears, there may be a surprise inside…
or you might find your greatest gift.

Little known facts:
• Walt Disney was afraid of mice.

- Barbra Streisand and Cher suffered from stage fright.

I was afraid of public speaking. I do it all the time now to promote my books.

Recognize that there is much to be gained from facing your fear.

RECOGNIZE
that happiness is a state of mind.

On happiness:

"Happiness is a butterfly, which, when pursued, is always just beyond your grasp, but which, if you will sit down quietly, may alight upon you."
– Nathaniel Hawthorne

"Success is getting what you want. Happiness is liking what you get." – H. Jackson Brown

"The foolish man seeks happiness in the distance, the wise grows it under his feet." – James Oppenheim

"The place to be happy is here, the time to be happy is now." – Robert Ingersoll

"People are just as happy as they make up their minds to be." – Abraham Lincoln

"The mind is its own place, and in itself, can make a Heaven of Hell and a Hell of Heaven." – John Milton

Life

"Our happiness depends on the habit of mind we cultivate. So, practice happy thinking every day. Cultivate the merry heart, develop the happiness habit, and life will become a continual feast."
– Norman Vincent Peale

"Happiness depends on ourselves." – Aristotle

"Seek first the Kingdom of Heaven and all else will be added unto you. The Kingdom of Heaven is within." – Jesus of Nazareth

"Happiness makes up in height what it lacks in length." – Robert Frost

"The purpose of our lives is to be happy." – Dalai Lama

When is it for you? When are you going to be happy? When you graduate? When you leave home? When you're on your own? When you get a job in Corporate America? When you get married? When you have a child? When you have another child? When you get divorced? When you get your degree? When you get that promotion? When you win the lottery? When your book gets published? When Hollywood buys the rights to your screenplay? When you retire?

That's what I thought. At various stages in my own life, that's what I thought. But, the reality is your life is now. Continue to pursue your dreams but be happy now and appreciate what you do have. Just yesterday, I was cleaning my house because it had gotten seriously out of control (at least for me). I was grumpily vacuuming the stairs when I developed a stank attitude because here I was spending my day off cleaning. I have a relatively nice house, and it's fairly large.

So, here I was, spending my whole Saturday cleaning this big house, and then it occurred to me that there are a lot of people... truly a lot of people who would love to have my problem. And then I was better. And just giving myself that insight helped me to get through that moment.

Happiness is a State of Mind.

Decide to be happy and you will be. Decide to have a stank attitude and that's exactly what you'll have, a stank attitude. States of mind tend to reproduce themselves, negative or positive. But, if it's negative, you can decide to break out of it.

But, even though I'd had the first experience, it must be realized that consciousness is a continuous, on-going process. It's about reminding yourself to rise to a certain state of consciousness, which in turn, brings awareness... and ultimately, peace and joy.

But, this revelation does not always have to come from you; sometimes it's from an outside source. You just have to be perceptive enough to recognize it.

"Goose-Goose"

I kept stressing because I am now a single mom... and well... things are different now... While my children were visiting with their father over the weekend, I had a chance to clean up... at least a little bit. But as soon as they came home, the house was a mess again. I developed a "stank" attitude as a result. Not only was my house in a total state of disarray again, but here I was spending my Saturday—one of my only days off—cleaning it up... again. I went inward calling on peace and joy to envelop and comfort me, and shortly after that, a little cartoon came on that featured a little dog. The little dog ended up taking care of this little goose that had come to him under duress in the middle of the night. (Incidentally, I frequently call my daughters, goose-goose). Anyway, while running the vacuum cleaner, the little dog was complaining about what a mess the little goose was making when the vacuum cleaner suddenly ran over one of the toys that the little goose had strewn all over the floor. But the little dog didn't know that. He thought the vacuum cleaner had sucked up the little goose, as the goose was no where around. Needless to say, he was frantic, until the little goose came out of the back room toting more toys. Ecstatic and grateful that the little goose was safe, the dog ran and scooped the little goose up into his arms. I was paying attention. I got it.

Then the thought occurred to me that there are some people in this world who would love to have this problem – my problem. Again, I got the message.

But, this is true for you, too. Think about your life, there are people who would love to have what you have... wishing they had what you have. You have it and you're willing to throw it away looking for something better. As a consequence, some people might decide to take what you have, while you are busy looking for something else. Appreciate what you have.

Recognize that appreciation and happiness go hand in hand.

RECOGNIZE

that Life is an exquisite gift.

On life:

"Until you know that life is interesting – and find it so – you haven't found your soul." – Geoffrey Fisher

"It is not length of life, but depth of life."
– Ralph Waldo Emerson

"At the foundation of every life is one central desire: to make a difference that you lived." – Ron Smothermon

"There are four questions of value in life…
What is sacred? Of what is the spirit made?
What is worth living for, and what is worth dying for?
The answer to each is the same. Only love."
– Don Juan DeMarco

"You will find, as you look back upon your life, that the moments when you really lived are the moments when you have done things in the spirit of love."
– Henry Drummond

"Somebody should tell us, right at the start of our lives, that we are dying. Then we might live life to the limit, every minute of every day. Do it! I say. Whatever you want to do, do it now. There are only so many tomorrows." – Michael Landon

"Be here now." – Baba Ram Das

"Life isn't about the breaths we take, it's about the moments that take our breath away." – Unknown

"Life's a Trip!"

Life is a "trip." Literally, life is a "trip." It's a spiritual journey. It's a wild and perplexing ride, where sometimes we cruise blissfully under sunny, blue skies and then other times we are left to navigate the rough terrain of confusing twists and turns. If the road of life has you lost and you find yourself going around in circles, stop and seek some direction. Take the road within.

Life is a wonderful gift. And you are an exquisite, extraordinary work of art. Focus on the good in your Life and enjoy it!

Recognize that life is a trip, so let your spirit guide you.

"A human being is part of the whole, called by us "Universe"; a part limited in time and space. He experiences himself, his thoughts, and feelings as something separated from the rest- a kind of optical delusion of his consciousness. This delusion is a kind of prison for us, restricting us to our personal desires and to affection for a few persons nearest to us. Our task must be to free ourselves from this prison by widening our circle of compassion to embrace all living creatures, and the whole of nature in its beauty." - Albert Einstein

Wake Up

Awake

Conscious
Alert wakeful astir wide-eyed bright-eyed watchful
attentive sharp circumspect observant

Wake Up
Rouse
A rise
Arouse
Inspire
Inform

Asleep

Comatose
Inattentive
Dull
Off guard
Unconscious
In a slumber
Sleeping
In a sound sleep
Dreaming
Heavy with sleep

The universe is a powerful dynamic—all you have
to do is open yourself up to its energy. How?
Wake up to the Creator in You.

You Better Recognize!

You Better Recognize!

Directory
of Resources

Books for your-Self

Title	Author	ISBN
Conversations with God: Book One	Neale Donald Walsch	0-399-14278-9
Conversations with God: Book Two	Neale Donald Walsch	1-57174-056-2
Conversations with God: Book Three	Neale Donald Walsch	1-57174-103-8
Friendship with God	Neale Donald Walsch	0-399-14541-9
How to Know God	Deepak Chopra, M.D.	0-609-60078-8
Creating Affluence: The A-to-Z Steps to a Richer Life	Deepak Chopra, M.D.	1-878424-34-3
The Seat of the Soul	Gary Zukav	0-671-69507-X
The Art of Happiness: A Handbook for Living	His Holiness the Dalai Lama and Howard C. Cutler, M.D.	1-57322-111-2
The Four Agreements	Miguel Ruiz	0-965-046365
Who Moved My Cheese? An A-mazing Way to Deal with Change in Your Work and in Your Life	Spencer Johnson, M.D.	0-399-14446-3
The Blue Light	Walter Mosley	0-446-60692-8
Why Meditate?	Clint Willis (editor)	156924586X
Get Off Your Assets!	Desi Willamson	0-7872-6620-5
Living the 7 Habits: The Courage to Change	Stephen R. Covey	0-684-85716-2
The 7 Habits of Highly Effective People	Stephen R. Covey	
Radiant Women of Color	Gracie Cornish	0-9630654-1-6
Men Are From Mars Women Are From Venus	John Gray, Ph.D.	0-06-019132-5
Chicken Soup for the Soul (Series)	Jack Canfield	1-55874-812-1

Resources

Title	Author	ISBN
Chicken Soup for the Little Souls	Mark Victor Hansen Lisa McCourt	1-55874-812-1
The Silent Miracle	Ron Rathbun	0-425-16678-3
Awakening Your True Spiritual Nature By Stilling Your Mind	Ron Rathbun	0-425-16678-3
The Way is Within	Ron Rathbun	
It's Not Over Until You Win!	Les Brown see: http://www.lesbrown.com/	
Live Your Dreams	Les Brown see: http://www.lesbrown.com/	
The Little Engine that Could		
Death Does Not Exist	Elizabeth Kubler-Ross, M.D.	
On Death and Dying	Elizabeth Kubler-Ross, M.D.	0684839385
Death: The Final Stage of Growth	Elizabeth Kubler-Ross, M.D.	0684839415
The Dark Side of the Light Chasers	Deborah Ford	
Chinese Herbal Medicine	Daniel P. Reid	
Men are from Mars Women are from Venus	Dr. John Gray	0-06-019132-5
Selling You	Napoleon Hill	0-940687-29-1
Believe and Achieve	Napoleon Hill	0-940687-45-3
The Science of Personal Achievement	Napoleon Hill	0-671-86996-5
Key's to Success: The 17 Principles of Personal Achievement	Napoleon Hill	1-55927-391-7
The Master-Key to Riches & Grow Rich with Peace of Mind	Napoleon Hill	1-55935-296-5
Think and Grow Rich	Napoleon Hill	0-940687-00-3
Don't Sweat the Small Stuff About Money	Richard Carlson, Ph.D.	0-7868-8637-4
Think Yourself Rich	Joseph Murphy, Ph.D, .D.D.	0-7352-0223-0

Movies for your-Self

Movie Title	Actors	Comments
As Good As It Gets	Jack Nicolson, Helen Hunt, Cuba Gooding Jr.	Recognize the light in others.
Joe vs. the Volcano	Tom Hanks, Meg Ryan	Recognize that if you are afraid to live your life, you will be afraid to *live* your life.
Patch Adams	Robin Williams	Recognize the healing properties of laughter.
Forrest Gump	Tom Hanks, Sally Fields, Mykelti Williams	Recognize the beauty of innocence.
Grand Canyon	Danny Glover, Alfre Woodard	Recognize that the life experience is a communal experience.

Resources

Websites for your-Self

Topic	URL
The healing properties of laughter.	http://www.rxlaughter.org/ and http://members.aol.com/shrinkchat/humor.htm
Interesting Quotes	http://www.geocities.com/wrightflyer2/personalthoughts.html http://www.geocities.com/wrightflyer2/
Memo from God	http://www.webspirations.net/memo/
Webinspirations	http://www.webspirations.net/index.htm
Interview with God	http://www.webspirations.net/interview/
The Road to Success	http://www.webspirations.net/roadto/
I Believe I Can Fly	http://www.kirstimd.com/icanfly.htm
Imagine	http://www.merseyworld.com/imagine/lyrics/imagine.htm
THE MEDITATION ARCHIVE	http://www.interluderetreat.com/medarc.htm
ACCEPT THE POSSIBILITY: Interview with Neale Donald Walsh (author of Conversations with God)	http://www.cogenesis.com/journal/virtualalexandria/interlog/walsh.html
Stress Management and Relaxation at 9to5café.com: Online Relaxation Mood Rooms include: Wild horses running free, Seacam Fish Tank, Fractal Trip, Sea, Nature, Astral, Zen and Psychedelic	http://www.9to5cafe.com/Home/Relax/relax_homepage.htm http://www.9to5cafe.com/

Audio and Video Programs for your-Self

Title	Author	How to Order
The Higher Self: The Magic of Inner and Outer Fulfillment	Deepak Chopra, M.D.	1-800-525-9000 www.nightingale.com
Rich Dad Secrets To Money, Business and Investing... and How You can Profit from Them	Robert T. Kiyosaki	1-800-525-9000 www.nightingale.com
The Power of Purpose How to Create The Life You Always Wanted Sell Your Way to Greatness You Deserve! It's Possible The Power to Change Live Your Dreams... Get Past Your Fears Take Charge of Your Life Les Brown Speaks At The T.D. Jakes Manpower Conf.	Les Brown	see: http:// www.lesbrown.com/ - or - 1-800-525-9000 www.nightingale.com

Magazines for your-Self

Title	Contact
"O"	The Oprah Magazine PO Box 7831 Red Oak, IA 51591-2831 http://www.oprah.com/ omagazineomag_subscribe.jhtml
"New Age"	New Age PO Box 1949 Marion, OH 43306-2049 http://www.newage.com/ To get a free copy of the magazine, visit: https://www.kable.com/najr/subDom.asp
"Open Minds"	Open Minds, Inc. PO Box 546 Adams, WI 53910 608-339-3783
"Essence" ("In the Spirit" segment)	Essence PO Box 51300 Boulder, Colorado 80323-1300
"Self Healing"	1-800-523-3296 To get a free copy of the magazine, visit: https://www.drweilselfhealing.com/ free_issue.asp or Write: Dr. Andrew Weil's Self Healing P. O. Box 2057 Marion, OH 43306-2157

Art for your-Self

Title	Artist
"Sankofa Collection"	Norman A. Hughes
"Positive Image Collection"	http://www.littleafrica.com/sankofa/
	http://www.the-webstore.com/
	figurines/sankofa/sankofa_
	menu.htm

Positive Images

Spirit Guides

Kurt Runstadler
Runstadler Studios, Inc.
6549 Stanley Ave.
Carmichael, CA 95608
See also: www.spiritguides.net

Music for your-Self

People tend to think when it comes to spirituality, there's only one kind of music and everything else is tossed into the "secular" category. But much of the music that has been tossed into this category speaks loudly to the soul. And isn't that what spirituality is all about?

Cut	Artist	CD Title
Entire CD	Iyanla Vanzant with various artists	"In the Meantime"
"Open Your Mind" "It's a New Day" "Because of You" "Change the Outcome" *For more on Terry visit:* *http://www.terrybradford.com/ Infin/bradford_bio.htm* *http://www.terrybradford.com/ indexog2.htm*	Terry Bradford	"Terry Bradford Live! The Experience"
"Hero" *(For lyrics see: http://members.aol.com/ pwyatt1111/herolyrics.html)*	Mariah Carey	"Hero", Music Box Mariah Carey: No. 1's
"Make It Happen"	Mariah Carey	"Mariah Carey MTV Unplugged EP"
"All I Ever Ask"	Najee/ Freddie Jackson	"Love Songs"
"Just An Illusion"	Najee	"Just An Illusion"
"Higher"	Creed	"Human Clay"
"Ascension (Don't Ever Wonder)"	Maxwell	"Maxwell's Urban Hang Suite"

Cut	Artist	CD Title
"Gestation Mythos" "I'm You: You Are Me" "Drown Deep: Hula" "Submerge: 'Til We Become The Sun" "Embrya"	Maxwell	"Embrya"
"Just You 'n' Me"	Chicago	"Chicago's Greatest Hits"

"Does Anybody
   Really Know
   What Time It Is?"
	Chicago	"Chicago's Greatest
		   Hits"

"Beginnings"	Chicago	"Chicago's Greatest Hits"
"Purple Rain"	Prince	"Purple Rain"
"Mahogany"	Diana Ross	"Mahogany" Soundtrack/Movie

"Keep Your Head
   To The Sky"
"Fantasy"
"Shining Star"
	Earth, Wind
	and Fire
		"Best of Earth, Wind,
		   and Fire" Vol.2
		"That's the Way of
		   the World"
		   (Remaster)

"The Miseducation
   of Lauryn Hill"
"Lost Ones"
"Everything
   is Everything"
	Lauryn Hill	"The Miseducation
		   of Lauryn Hill"

"We Are One" "Joy and Pain"	Frankie Beverly and Maze	"Maze: Anthology" Maze/Beverly Live In New Orleans "We are One"

Resources

Cut	Artist	CD Title
"I'll Be There"	Michael Jackson or Mariah Carey	"Mariah Carey MTV Unplugged EP" "Mariah Carey: No. 1's"
"The Greatest Love of All"	George Benson or Whitney Houston	"The Best of George Benson" "Whitney Houston"
"Imagine" *For lyrics visit: http:// www.merseyworld.com/ imagine/lyrics/ imagine.htm*	John Lennon	"Imagine" John Lennon Anthology
"I Believe I Can Fly" *For lyrics visit: http:// www.kirstimd.com/ icanfly.htm*	R. Kelly	"I Believe I Can Fly"
"Higher Love"	Steve Winwood Chaka Khan	
"I Hope You Dance"	Lee Ann Womack	"I Hope You Dance"
"My Favorite Things"	Luther Vandross (Also by various artists)	"This is Christmas"

Financial Freedom for your-Self

Resource Type	Title	URL/ISBN
Website	NAIC (National Association of Investors Corporation)	http://www.better-investing.com/
Website	American Association of Individual Investors: Investing Basics	http://www.aaii.org/invbas/index.shtml
Website	The Street.com Investing Basics	http://www.thestreet.com/basics/
Website	Free business cards	http://www.vistaprint.com
Websites	Other Resources:	http://www.brooke stephens.com
		http://www.datachimp.com/articles/financials/fundamentals.htm
		http://www.valueline.com/vlu/4-index.html
		http://www.consumer quote.com/
		http://www.richdad.com/
Book	*Get Off Your Assets!* Desi Williamson	0-7872-6620-5
Book	*Creating Affluence: The A-to-Z Steps to a Richer Life* Deepak Chopra, M.D.	1-878424-34-3
	Rich Dad, Poor Dad Robert T. Kiyosaki	0446677450

Resources

Resource Type	Title	URL/ISBN
Book	*Wealth Happens One Day At A Time* Brooke M. Stephens	0-88730-982-8
Credit Bureau Contact	**Equifax** Equifax Credit Information Services, Inc. P.O. Box 740241 Atlanta, GA 30374 1-800-685-1111	http://www.equifax.com
Credit Bureau Contact	1 888 EXPERIAN (1 888 397 3742) Or send a written request with a check or money order to: Experian PO Box 2002 Allen, TX 75013-2002	http://www.experian.com/
Credit Bureau Contact	TransUnion LLC Consumer Disclosure Center P.O. Box 1000 Chester, PA 19022 Call 800-888-4213	http://www.tuc.com/
Credit Bureau Contact	3 BureauReport.com	http://www.3bureau report.com/
Social Security Admin. (fraud line)	1-800-269-0271	
You can get free business cards at		www.vistaprint.com

Energy for your-Self

Ingredients:

2 Tsp lemon juice (1/2 a lemon or use Minute Maid Frozen
Lemon Juice in the black and yellow box)
1/2 cup of distilled water (it can be warm)
2 Tsp of PURE maple syrup (not imitation)
A pinch of red, cayenne pepper

The above recipe was given to me for energy and circulation.
But, I tend to use a lot more lemon juice, maple syrup, and
red pepper. I usually put it in the microwave oven and drink
it like tea.

Poetry for your-Self

Chocolate Jewels
by
Valerie Rose

mommy's chocolate jewels
mmm... sweet, delectable
sun-kissed skin
the light of my life
what will you do?
what will be your gift to the universe?

mommy's chocolate jewels
mmm... good! good! good!
rainbow flesh
mommy's joy
the fruit of my existence
two chocolate stars
from the heavens
two precious gifts
from the universe

(Untitled – On Death)
Author Unknown

Do not stand at my grave and weep;
I am not there, I do not sleep.
I am a thousand winds that blow;
I am the diamond glints of snow.
I am the sunlight on ripened grain;
I am the gentle autumn's rain.
When you awaken in the morning's hush,
I am the swift uplifting rush
Of quiet birds in circled flight.
I am the soft star that shines at night.
Do not stand at my grave and cry;
I am not there; I did not die.

The Right Thing
by
Valerie Rose

did i do the right thing?
i wonder
children murdered,
senselessly
but then
i
look
into
your
face
and i see mine
your eyes shine
with the innocent joy
of being alive
did i do the right thing?
i ask myself
freaks in the neighborhood
afraid to let you out of my sight
for more than fraction
afraid of what could happen
afraid to let you roam freely
as your youth would lead you to do
your wings are clipped,
secured at the base at least
sorry,
but i have no choice
not really
but then,
your
open,
uninhibited
laughter

(cont.)

once
again
is
the
sunrise
of
my
soul
but did i do the right thing?
depleting ozone
diminishing forests
and the landfills are full
but then,
suddenly,
there were two,
two sets of dancing eyes
two joyous delights
unbridled belly laughs times two
reflections of myself
but did i do the right thing?
the question still haunts me
atrocities of war
the simple,
yet inevitable
pain of life
and then
the universe whispers
softly in my ear
that it was you who made the choice
not i
it was you who chose me,
not the other way around
it was you all along
and i thank you,
i thank you for choosing me
i thank you
for bringing the joy
that you bring

In the Know
by
Valerie Rose

Build an igloo with me
Hold my hand
Chase me through the snow
Kiss me gently
Walk with me through an apple orchard in the fall
Listen to me
Eat popcorn with me at a slumber party for two
Hold me close
Stand barefoot with me at the edge of the crystal blue
Caribbean
Be quiet with me
Salsa with me at a fancy hotel
Have fun with me
Give me your attention
Respect me
Spend hours with me on the telephone for no reason at all
Talk to me
Horseback ride with me in the Spring through a field of
daffodils
Be sweet to me
Whisper your thoughts into my ear
Share with me
Talk to me
Breathe with me
Be
with me.

Flame Dance
by
Valerie Rose

the flame dances
to the silent melody
of mysteries
eternally

the flames dance
to the silent melodies
of mystery
eternally

the flame dances
to the silent melody
of mysteries
eternally...

Quotes for your-Self

On what lies within:

"You have to know that your real home is within."
– Quincy Jones

"We are not human beings having a spiritual experience; we are spiritual beings having a human experience." – Teilhard de Chardin

"What lies behind us and what lies before us are tiny matters compared to what lies within us."
– Ralph Waldo Emerson

"We dance round in a ring and suppose, But the Secret sits in the middle and knows." – Robert Frost

"Look within!... The secret is inside you." – Hui-neng

"I suppose what makes me most glad is that we all recognize each other in this metaphysical space of silence and happening, and get some sense, for a moment, that we are full of paradise without knowing it." – Thomas Merton

On humanity:

"We are all citizens of one world, we are all of one blood. To hate a man because he was born in another country, because he speaks a different language, or because he takes a different view on this subject or that, is a great folly. Desist, I implore you, for we are all equally human. Let us have but one end in view, the welfare of humanity."
– Johann Amos Comenius

"Wherever there is a human being, there is an opportunity for kindness." – Seneca

"Be kind, remember everyone you meet is fighting a hard battle." – T.H. Thompson

"Beginning today, treat everyone you meet as if they were going to be dead by midnight. Extend to them all the care, kindness, and understanding you can muster, and do it with no thought of any reward. Your life will never be the same again." – Og Mandino

On becoming a business owner:

"I am a woman who came from the cotton fields of the South. I was promoted from there to the washtub. Then I was promoted to the kitchen cook, and from there I promoted myself into the business of manufacturing hair good and preparations."
– Madame C. J. Walker

On bitterness:

"If I have learned anything in my life, it is that bitterness consumes the vessel that contains it."
– Ruben "Hurricane" Carter

On success:

"Success isn't measured by the position you reach in life, it's measured by the obstacles you overcome."
– Booker T. Washington

On laughter:

"A smile that burst." – Patricia Nelson

"A universal bond that draws all men closer."
– Nathan Ausubel.

"A tranquilizer with no side effects." – Arnold Glasow

"We shall never know all the good that a simple
smile can do." – Mother Teresa

On judging:

"If you judge people you have no time to love them."
– Mother Teresa

"Sweep first before your own door before you sweep
the doorsteps of your neighbors." – Swedish Proverb

"We should be lenient in our judgment, because
often the mistakes of others would have been ours
had we had the opportunity to make them."
– Dr. Alsaker

On idleness:

"Take rest; a field that has rested gives a beautiful
crop." – Ovid

"If you can spend a perfectly useless afternoon in a
perfectly useless manner, you have learned how to
live." – Lin Yutang

"Sit quietly, doing nothing, spring comes, and the grass grows by itself." – Zen Saying

"How beautiful it is to do nothing, and then rest afterward." – Spanish Proverb

"The time you enjoy wasting is not wasted time."
– Bertrand Russell

On actions:

"We cannot live only for ourselves. A thousand fibers connect us with our fellow men; and among those fibers, as sympathetic threads, our actions run as causes, and they come back to us as effects."
– Herman Melville

"Everything you do, and everything you don't do, has an effect." – Kenneth & Linda Schatz

"In nature there are neither rewards nor punishments — there are only consequences."
– Robert Green Ingersoll

"If you see good in people, you radiate a harmonious loving energy which uplifts those who are around you. If you can maintain this habit, this energy will turn into a steady flow of love."
– Annamalai Swami

On consequences:

> "Life does not require us to be consistent, cruel, patient, helpful, angry, rational, thoughtless, loving, rash, open-minded, neurotic, careful, rigid, tolerant, wasteful, rich, downtrodden, gentle, sick, considerate, funny, stupid, healthy, greedy, beautiful, lazy, responsive, foolish, sharing, pressured, intimate, hedonistic, industrious, manipulative, insightful, capricious, wise, selfish, kind or sacrificed. Life does, however, require us to live with the consequences of our choices." – Richard Bach

On taking control:

> "The thought you have now shapes your experience of the next moment. Practice shaping the moment."
> – Tom Barrett

> "It may take practice to think more positively and more compassionately, but just as you must train a puppy to behave the way you want it to, you must train your mind to behave itself. Otherwise, like the puppy, your mind will just make a lot of messes."
> – Tom Barrett

On adversity:

> "If I had a formula for bypassing trouble, I would not pass it round. Trouble creates a capacity to handle it. I don't embrace trouble; that's as bad as treating it as an enemy. But I do say meet it as a friend, for you'll see a lot of it and had better be on speaking terms with it." – Oliver Wendell Holmes

"Adversity causes some men to break; others to break records." – William A. Ward

"Adversity is like a strong wind. It tears away from us all but the things that cannot be torn, so that we see ourselves as we really are." – Arthur Golden

On role models:

"The most important role models in people's lives, it seems, aren't superstars or household names. They're 'everyday' people who quietly set examples for you — coaches, teachers, parents. People about whom you say to yourself, perhaps not even consciously, 'I want to be like that.'" – Tim Foley

"Some of the most important people in my life would be shocked to learn that they were role models. They weren't celebrities, or even particularly accomplished. But they had some quality that I admired, that made me want to be like them."
– Donn Moomaw

"You don't have to know people personally for them to be role models. Some of my most important role models were historical or literary figures that I only read about — never actually met." – John Wilson

On appreciation:

"One we discover how to appreciate the timeless values in our daily experiences, we can enjoy the best things in life." – Harry Hepner

Resources

"Prosperity depends more on wanting what you have than having what you want." – Geoffrey F. Abert

On the dream of life:

"Your vision will become clear only when you look into your heart… Who looks outside, dreams. Who looks inside, awakens." – Carl Jung

"We sometimes congratulate ourselves at the moment of waking from a troubled dream… it may be so at the moment of death." – Nathaniel Hawthorne

On peace:

"Liberty in tranquility." – Cicero

On happiness:

"Happiness is a butterfly, which, when pursued, is always just beyond your grasp, but which, if you will sit down quietly, may alight upon you."
– Nathaniel Hawthorne

"Success is getting what you want. Happiness is liking what you get." – H. Jackson Brown

"The place to be happy is here, the time to be happy is now." – Robert Ingersoll

"People are just as happy as they make up their minds to be." – Abraham Lincoln

"The mind is its own place, and in itself, can make a Heaven of Hell and a Hell of Heaven." – John Milton

157

"Our happiness depends on the habit of mind we cultivate. So, practice happy thinking every day. Cultivate the merry heart, develop the happiness habit, and life will become a continual feast."
– Norman Vincent Peale

"Happiness depends on ourselves." – Aristotle

"Seek first the Kingdom of Heaven and all else will be added unto you. The Kingdom of Heaven is within." – Jesus of Nazareth

"Happiness makes up in height what it lacks in length." – Robert Frost

"The purpose of our lives is to be happy." – Dalai Lama

"Until you know that life is interesting – and find it so – you haven't found your soul." – Geoffrey Fisher

"It is not length of life, but depth of life."
– Ralph Waldo Emerson

"At the foundation of every life is one central desire: to make a difference that you lived." – Ron Smothermon

"There are four questions of value in life... What is sacred? Of what is the spirit made? What is worth living for, and what is worth dying for? The answer to each is the same. Only love." – Don Juan DeMarco

"You will find, as you look back upon your life, that the moments when you really lived are the moments when you have done things in the spirit of love."
– Henry Drummond

"Somebody should tell us, right at the start of our lives, that we are dying. Then we might live life to the limit, every minute of every day. Do it! I say. Whatever you want to do, do it now. There are only so many tomorrows." – Michael Landon

"Be here now." – Baba Ram Das

"Life isn't about the breaths we take, it's about the moments that take our breath away." – Unknown

"Life isn't about finding yourself. Life is about creating yourself." – George Bernard Shaw

"It is wonderful how much time good people spend fighting the devil. If they would only expend the same amount of energy loving their fellow men, the devil would die in his own tracks of ennui."
– Helen Keller

"Ask yourself whether the dream of heaven and greatness should be waiting for us in our graves – or whether it should be ours here and now and on this earth." – Ayn Rand

"How far you go in life depends on your being tender with the young, compassionate with the aged, sympathetic with the striving, and tolerant of the weak and strong. Because someday in your life you will have been all of these." – George Washington Carver

"Ancient Egyptians believed that upon death they would be asked two questions and their answers would determine whether they could continue their journey in the afterlife. The first question was, "Did you bring joy?" The second was, "Did you find joy?"
– Leo Buscaglia

"I have Died many a death in love, and yet, had I not loved I would never have lived at all." – David Lasater

"The bitterest tears shed over graves are for words left unsaid and deeds left undone."
– Harriet Beecher Stowe

"Yesterday is ashes; tomorrow wood. Only today does the fire burn brightly." – Old Eskimo saying

"This is the day which the Lord has made. Let us rejoice and be glad in it." – Psalms

"Do not worry about tomorrow's trouble, for you do not know what the day may bring. Tomorrow may come and you will be no more, and so you will have worried about a world that is not yours."
– Babylonian Talmud

On creation:

"To be alive, to be able to see, to walk… it's all a miracle. I have adopted the technique of living life from miracle to miracle." – Arthur Rubinstein

"Earth's crammed with Heaven."
– Elizabeth Barrett Browning

"My father says that almost everyone is asleep… There are only a few people who are really awake. And those people live in a constant state of amazement." – paraphrased, Meg Ryan in the movie *Joe Vs. the Volcano*

"You say grace before meals. All right. But I say grace before the concert and the opera, and grace before the play and pantomime, and grace before I open a book, and grace before sketching, painting, swimming, fencing, boxing, walking, playing, dancing, and grace before I dip the pen in the ink."
– G.K. Chesterton

On forgiveness:

"Bitterness imprisons life; love releases it."
– Henry Emerson Fosdick

"People are often unreasonable, illogical and self-centered; Forgive them anyway."
– Mother Teresa of Calcutta

"When I am able to resist the temptation to judge others, I can see them as teachers of forgiveness in my life, reminding me that I can only have peace of mind when I forgive rather than judge."
– Gerald Jampolsky

On love:

"Our highest word, and the synonym for God."
—Ralph Waldo Emerson

"Friendship set on fire." – Jeremy Taylor

"The heart's immortal thirst to be completely known and all forgiven." – Henry Van Dyke

"Spiritual fire." – Emanuel Swedenborg

"Two minds without a single thought." – Philip Barry

"Love is what's in the room with you at the holidays if you stop opening presents and listen." – Bobby, age 5

"If you want to learn to love better, you should start with a friend who you hate." – Nikka, age 6

"Love is like a little old woman and a little old man who are still friends even after they know each other so well." – Tommy, age 6

"Love is when mommy sees daddy on the toilet and she doesn't think it's gross." – Mark, age 6

"You really shouldn't say 'I love you' unless you mean it. But if you mean it, you should say it a lot. People forget." – Jessica, age 8

On creativity:

"Every human is an artist. The dream of your life is to make beautiful art." – don Miguel Ruiz

"You have only one source of creativity – your own unique talents, skills, perspectives, and experiences. You can't be creative with someone else's stuff, because creativity, by definition, is the process of translating who you are into some outward manifestation. It doesn't matter whether that is a painting, an ad campaign, a holiday dinner, a business report, or the raising of a healthy child. The creative process can be applied to all of our activities, eventually yielding a truly creative life."
– G. Lynne Snead and Joyce Wycoff

Resources

"Discontent translated into art." – Eric Hoffer

On life:

"A vapor that appeareth for a little time and then vanisheth away." – Bible

"A little gleam of time between two eternities." – Thomas Carlyle

"A play. It's not in its length, but its performance that counts." – Seneca.

"Be here now." – Baba Ram Das

"Somebody should tell us, right at the start of our lives, that we are dying. Then we might live life to the limit, every minute of every day. Do it! I say. Whatever you want to do, do it now. There are only so many tomorrows." – Michael Landon

"Life is what happens while you are making other plans." – John Lennon

On creation:

"Every tree and plant in the meadow seemed to be dancing, those which average eyes would see as fixed and still." – Rumi

"There are only two ways to live your life. One is as though nothing is a miracle. The other is as if everything is a miracle." – Albert Einstein

On living:

"Every man dies. Not every man really lives."
– William Wallace [From the movie *Braveheart*]

"If you had the choice between killing yourself and doing the thing that you're really afraid of, why not do the thing that you're really afraid of?"
– paraphrased, Tom Hanks in the movie *Joe Vs. the Volcano*

"There is no goal better than this one: to know as you lie on your deathbed that you lived your true life, and you did whatever made you happy."
– Steve Chandler, *"100 Ways to Motivate Yourself"*

Ancient Egyptians believed that upon death they would be asked two questions and their answers would determine whether they could continue their journey in the afterlife. The first question was, "Did you bring joy?" The second was, "Did you find joy?"
– Leo Buscaglia

On the notion that your life is now:

"Seize the moment. Remember all those women on the Titanic who waved off the dessert cart."
– Erma Bombeck, American Humorist

"Begin doing what you want to do now. We are not living in eternity. We have only this moment, sparkling like a star in our hand and melting like a snowflake." – Marie Beyon Ray

"Why not seize the pleasure at once? How often is happiness destroyed by preparation? Foolish preparation?" – Jane Austen

"Shoot for the moon. Even if you miss it you will land among the stars." – Les Brown

"You must be the change you wish to see in the world." – Mohandas Ghandi

"If you are going to walk on thin ice, you might as well dance." – Anonymous

"It Don't Mean a Thing If It Ain't Got That Swing." – Duke Ellington

"Anything I've ever done that ultimately was worthwhile… initially scared me to death." – Betty Bender

On death:

"Death is not extinguishing the light; it is putting out the lamp because dawn has come". – Rabindranath Tagore

"When the soul shall emerge from its sheath." – Marcus Aurelius

"The undiscovered country." – William Shakespeare

"Is death the last sleep? No – it is the last and final awakening." – Sir Walter Scott

"Don't grieve. Anything you lose comes round in another form." – Rumi

"I look upon death to be as necessary to the constitution as sleep. We shall rise refreshed in the morning." – Benjamin Franklin

"Our birth is but a sleep and a forgetting; The Soul that rises with us, our life's Star, Hath had elsewhere its setting. And cometh from afar." – William Wordsworth

"You see that who you are isn't moving in time. Time is describing the incarnations, the packing changes." – Ram Dass

"Know, therefore, that from the greater silence I shall return... Forget not that I shall come back to you... A little while, a moment of rest upon the wind, and another woman shall bear me." – Kahlil Gibran

"Who says the eternal being does not exist? Who says the sun has gone out? Someone who climbs up on the roof and closes his eyes tight, and says, I don't see anything." – Jalalu'l-din Rumi

"It is the secret of the world that all things subsist and do not die, but only retire a little from sight and afterwards return again. Nothing is dead; men feign themselves dead, and endure mock funerals... and there they stand looking out of the window, sound and well, in some strange new disguise." – Ralph Waldo Emerson

"It is no more surprising to be born once than to be born twice: everything in nature is resurrection." – Francois Voltaire

"It is a strong proof of men knowing most things before birth, that when mere children they grasp innumerable facts with such speed as to show that they are not then taking them in for the first time, but are remembering and recalling them." – Marcus Tullius Cicero

Resources

"I hold that when a person dies, his Soul returns again to earth; Arrayed in some new flesh-disguise, another mother gives him birth. With sturdier limbs and brighter brain, the old Soul takes the road again." – John Masefield

"Everything science has taught me strengthens my belief in the continuity of our spiritual existence after death. I believe in an immortal soul. Science has proved that nothing disintegrates into nothingness. Life and soul, therefore, cannot disintegrate into nothingness, and so are immortal."
– Werner von Braun

"The soul is immortal- well then, if I shall always live, I must have lived before, lived for a whole eternity."
– Leo Tolstoy

"The tomb is not a blind alley: it is a thoroughfare. It closes on the twilight. It opens on the dawn."
– Victor Hugo

"The soul of man is like to water; from Heaven it cometh, to Heaven it riseth... And then returning to earth, forever alternating." – Johann Wolfgang von Goethe

"My life often seemed to me like a story that has no beginning and no end. I had the feeling that I was an historical fragment, an excerpt for which the preceding and succeeding text was missing. I could well imagine that I might have lived in former centuries and there encountered questions I was not yet able to answer; that I had been born again because I had not fulfilled the task given to me."
– Carl Jung

On adversity:

"In the middle of difficulty lies opportunity."
– Albert Einstein

"When written in Chinese, the word crisis is composed of two characters. One represents danger, and the other represents opportunity."
– John F. Kennedy

"In the depth of winter, I finally learned that there was in me an invincible summer." – Albert Camus

On persistence:

"Obstacles are those frightful things you see when you take your eyes off your goals." – unknown

"Our greatest glory is not in never failing, but in rising up every time we fail." – Ralph Waldo Emerson

"It is not because things are difficult that we do not dare, it is because we do not dare that they are difficult." – Seneca

"The heights by great men reached and kept were not obtained by sudden flight. But they, while their companions slept, were toiling upward in the night."
– Thomas S. Monson

"If the going is real easy, beware, you may be headed down hill." – unknown

"Never, never, never give up." – Winston Churchill

On success:

"The reward of toil." – Sophocles

On negativity:

"People deal too much with the negative, with what is wrong. Why not try and see positive things, to just touch those things and make them bloom?"
– Thich Nhat Hanh

"I will not let anyone walk through my mind with their dirty feet!" – Mahatma Gandhi

On success:

"Not the result of spontaneous combustion. You must set yourself on fire." – Reginald Leach

On action:

"Well done is better than well said." – Ben Franklin

"Deeds are better than words are. Actions mightier than boastings." – Henry Wadsworth Longfellow

"Action may not always bring happiness; but there is no happiness without action." – Benjamin Disraeli

On dreams:

"Now is the operative word. Everything you put in your way is just a method of putting off the hour when you could actually be doing your dream. You don't need endless time and perfect conditions. Do it now. Do it today. Do it for twenty minutes and watch your heart start beating." – Barbara Sher

"I have learned this at least by my experiment: if one advances confidently in the direction of his dreams, and endeavors to live the life he has imagined, he will meet with a success unexpected in common hours." – Henry David Thoreau

"You eat in dreams, the custard of the day."
– Alexander Pope

"Make visible what, without you, might perhaps never been seen." – Robert Bresson

On visualization:

"Most of us visualize on a daily basis, but we often do it unconsciously and in a negative fashion. It is called worrying. What happens to our bodies when we worry? We tense up, disrupt our normal breathing, and psycho-physically prepare ourselves for failure. Instead, learn to use positive visualization to prepare yourself for success. As you do you will transform the energy that supports your worrying into fuel for making your dreams come true."
– Michael Gelb and Tony Buzan

On opportunity:

"Opportunity is missed by most people because it is dressed in overalls and looks like work."
– Thomas Alva Edison

"A pessimist sees the difficulty in every opportunity; an optimist sees the opportunity in every difficulty."
– Sir Winston Churchill

On failure:

"The highway to success" – John Keats

"Not the falling down, but the staying down."
– Mary Pickford

"In the middle of difficulty lies opportunity."
– Albert Einstein

"Many people dream of success. To me, success can only be achieved through repeated failure and introspection." – Soichiro Honda, founder of Honda Motors

On happiness:

"Happiness is as a butterfly which, when pursued, is always beyond our grasp, but which if you will sit down quietly, may alight upon you."
– Nathaniel Hawthorne

"Happiness depends upon ourselves." – Aristotle

"To live happily is an inward power of the soul."
– Marcus Aurelius

"It is all within yourself, in your way of thinking."
– Marcus Aurelius

On spring:

"A true reconstructionist." – Henry Timrod

On summer:

"Days dripping away like honey off a spoon."
– Wallace Stegner

On autumn:

"A second spring, when every leaf's a flower."
– Albert Camus

On winter:

"Trees stooping under burdens of snow, window
filigreed with frost, shadows of drifting hummocks
turning blue-cold as northerners mummify
themselves in coats and scarves." – Henry Clayborne

On everything:

"Some men see things as they are and say why; I
dream things that never were and say why not."
– Robert Kennedy

"Your living is determined not so much by what life
brings to you as by the attitude you bring to life; not
so much by what happens to you as by the way your
mind looks at what happens. Circumstances and
situations do color life but you have been given the
mind to choose what the color shall be."
– John Homer Miller

"The Kingdom of Heaven is within you... Seek ye
first the Kingdom of Heaven and all things will be
added unto you." – Jesus of Nazareth

"The way is not in the sky. The way is in the heart."
– Buddha, from The Dhammapada

"I saw sorrow turning to clarity." – Yoko Ono

"No man is rich enough to buy back his past."
– Oscar Wilde

"Yesterday is history. Tomorrow is a mystery. And today? Today is a gift. That's why we call it The Present." – Babatunde Olatunji

"Don't grieve. Anything you lose comes round in another form." – Rumi

"In the hour of adversity be not without hope / For crystal rain falls from black clouds." – Persian Poem

"When we long for life without difficulties, remind us that oaks grow strong in contrary winds and diamonds are made under pressure." – Peter Marshall

"Sometimes I go about pitying myself /
And all the while I am being carried across the sky /
By beautiful clouds." – Ojibway Indian saying

"What the caterpillar calls the end of the world the master calls a butterfly." – Richard Bach

"What lies behind us and what lies before us are tiny matters compared to what lies within us."
– Ralph Waldo Emerson

"Use what talents you possess; the woods would be very silent if no birds sang except those that sang best." – Henry Van Dyke

"I have a body and I am more than my body. I have
emotions and I am more than my emotions.
I have a mind and I am more than my mind. I am a
center of pure consciousness and energy."
– The New Living Qabalah (Kabbalah as arranged by Will Parfitt)

Think "impossible" and dreams get discarded,
projects get abandoned, and hope for wellness is
torpedoed. But let someone yell the words "It's
possible," and resources we hadn't been aware of
come rushing in to assist us in our quest. I believe
we are all potentially brilliant and creative–but only
if we believe it, only if we have an attitude of positive
expectancy toward our ideas, and only if we act on
them. – Author: Greg Anderson

"Stop focusing on the problem. Look past the
problem so that you can find the solution."
– paraphrased from the movie *Patch Adams*

Everyone is a house with four rooms, a physical, a
mental, an emotional and a spiritual. Most of us
tend to live in one room most of the time, but unless
we go into every room, every day, even if only to
keep it aired, we are not a complete person.
– Indian Proverb

"We shall never know all the good that a simple
smile can do." – Mother Teresa

"Kindness in words creates confidence. Kindness in
thinking creates profoundness. Kindness in giving
creates love." – Lao-Tzu

"The greatest good you can do for another is not
just to share your riches, but to reveal to him his
own." – Benjamin Disraeli

Resources

"It is one of the most beautiful compensations of this life that no man can sincerely try to help another without helping himself."
– Ralph Waldo Emerson

"Life gets life. Energy creates energy. It is by spending oneself that one becomes rich."
– Sarah Bernhart

"If you want others to be happy, practice compassion. If you want to be happy, practice compassion." – The Dalai Lama

"The foolish man seeks happiness in the distance, the wise grows it under his feet." – James Oppenheim

"In the middle of difficulty lies opportunity."
– Albert Einstein

"When written in Chinese, the word crisis is composed of two characters. One represents danger, and the other represents opportunity."
– John F. Kennedy

"I saw sorrow turning to clarity." – Yoko Ono

"In the depth of winter, I finally learned that there was in me an invincible summer." – Albert Camus
"Chance is always powerful. Let your hook always be cast; in the pool where you least expect it, there will be fish." – Ovid

"Live! Yes! Life is a banquet and most suckers are starving to death." – Patrick Dennis, *"Auntie Mame"*

"Question: What do you see yourself doing five years from now? Answer: I have no idea. I've never had a career plan and never will. I just always make sure that I'm doing something I love at the moment, and I find out where it takes me. I float downriver, then I wake up and say, 'Oh, here I am. I've had a swell float.'" – Diane Sawyer, interviewed in *US Magazine*, September 1997

"The secret of health for both the mind and the body is not to mourn for the past, not to worry about the future, nor to anticipate troubles, but to live the present moment wisely and earnestly."
– Buddha

"Take your life in your own hands and what happens? A terrible thing: no one to blame."
– Erica Jong

"It is a painful thing to look at your own trouble and know that you yourself and no one else has made it."
– Sophocles, Ajax, c. 450 B.C.

"Self pity is our worst enemy and if we yield to it, we can never do anything wise in the world."
– Helen Keller

"Knowing others is wisdom, knowing yourself is Enlightenment." – Lao-Tzu

"If you do not ask yourself what it is you know, you will go on listening to others and change will not come because you will not hear your own truth."
– Saint Bartholomew

"We have what we seek, it is there all the time, and if we give it time, it will make itself known to us."
– Thomas Merton

"Faith in one's self… is the best and safest course."
– Michelangelo

"If one advances confidently in the direction of his dreams and endeavors to live the life which he has imagined, he will meet with a success unexpected in common hours." – Henry David Thoreau

"I finally figured out the only reason to be alive is to enjoy it." – Rita Mae Brown

"Often people attempt to live their lives backwards: they try to have more things, or more money in order to do more of what they want so that they will be happier. The way it actually works is the reverse. You must first be who you really are, then, do what you need to do, in order to have what you want."
– Margaret Young

"Happiness depends upon ourselves." – Aristotle

"To live happily is an inward power of the soul."
– Marcus Aurelius

"The Kingdom of Heaven is within you… Seek ye first the Kingdom of Heaven and all things will be added unto you." – Jesus of Nazareth

"The way is not in the sky. The way is in the heart." – Buddha, from The Dhammapada

"Joy has nothing to do with material things, or with man's outward circumstance…A man living in the lap of luxury can be wretched, and a man in the depths of poverty can overflow with joy."
– William Barcay

"The heights by great men reached and kept were not obtained by sudden flight. But they, while their companions slept, were toiling upward in the night."
– Thomas S. Monson

"To laugh often and much; to win the respect of intelligent people and the affection of children; to earn the appreciation of honest critics and to endure the betrayal of false friends; to appreciate beauty; to find the best in others; to leave the world a bit better whether by a healthy child, a garden patch or a redeemed social condition; to know even one life has breathed easier because you have lived. This is to have succeeded." – Ralph Waldo Emerson

"The trick is not how much pain you feel-but how much joy you feel. Any idiot can feel pain. Life is full of excuses to feel pain, excuses not to live, excuses, excuses, excuses." – Erica Jong

"The best way to cheer yourself up is to cheer everybody else up." – Mark Twain

"Life is part positive and part negative. Suppose you went to hear a symphony orchestra and all they played were the little happy high notes. Would you leave soon? Let me hear the rumble of the bass, the crash of the cymbals and the minor keys." – Jim Rohn

"Love is life and if you miss love, you miss life."
– Leo Buscaglia

"Do not believe in anything simply because you have heard it. Do not believe in anything simply because it is spoken and rumored by many. Do not believe in anything simply because it is found written in your religious books. Do not believe in anything merely on the authority of your teachers and elders. Do not believe in traditions because they have been handed down for many generations. But after observation and analysis, when you find that anything agrees with reason and is conducive to the good and benefit of one and all, then accept it and live up to it." – Buddha

"Spirit... is the point of human transcendence; It is the point where the human is open to the divine, that is, to the infinite and the eternal. It is also the point where human beings communicate. At that point of the Spirit, we are all open to one another." – Father Bede Griffiths

"There are only two ways to live your life. One is as though nothing is a miracle. The other is as if everything is a miracle." – Albert Einstein

"Drumsound rises on the air, its throb, my heart. A voice inside the beat says, I know you're tired, but come. This is the way." – Jeláluddín Rúmí

"The universe is full of magical things, patiently waiting for our wits to grow sharper." – Eden Phillpotts

"You can observe a lot by watching." – Yogi Berra

"The capacity for delight is the gift of paying attention." – Julia Cameron

"The mystical is not how the world is, but that it is." – Ludwig Wittgenstein

"One does not discover new lands without consenting to lose sight of the shore for a very long time." – André Gide

"A good traveler has no fixed plans, and is not intent on arriving." – Lao Tzu (570-490 B.C.)

"Wheresoever you go, go with all your heart."
– Confucius

"Avoiding danger is no safer in the long run than outright exposure. Life is either a daring adventure or nothing." – Helen Keller

"Do not go where the path may lead; go instead where there is no path and leave a trail."
– Ralph Waldo Emerson

"When you come to a fork in the road, take it."
– Yogi Berra

"Everything has its wonders, even darkness and silence, and I learn, whatever state I may be in, therein to be content." – Helen Keller

"Every wall is a door." – Emerson

"When it gets dark enough you can see the stars."
– Lee Salk

Resources

Bibliography

Books

Walsch, Neale Donald (1995). *Conversations with God: Book One,* NY: G. P. Putnam's Sons.

Walsch, Neale Donald (1997). *Conversations with God: Book Two,* VA: Hampton Roads Publishing Company Inc.

Walsch, Neale Donald (1998). *Conversations with God: Book Three,* VA: Hampton Roads Publishing Company Inc.

Walsch, Neale Donald (1999). *Friendship with God,* NY: G. P. Putnam's Sons.

Chopra M.D., Deepak (2000). *How to know God,* NY: Harmony Books/Crown Publishing.

Zukav, Gary (1989). *The Seat of the Soul,* NY: Fireside of Simon and Schuster Inc.

Dyer, Wayne W. (2001). *There's a Spiritual Solution to Every Problem,* NY: HarperCollins Publishers, Inc.

McCutcheon, March (1998). *Roget's SuperThesaurus – Marc McCutcheon,* OH: F&W Publications, Inc.

More Neighborly Thoughts from State Farm – Celebrating the African American Heritage State Farm Insurance

Johnson M.D., Spenser (1998). *Who Moved My Cheese? An A-mazing Way to Deal with Change in Your Work and in Your Life,* NY: G. P. Putnam's Sons

Chopra M.D., Deepak (1998). *Creating Affluence – The A-to-Z Steps to a Richer Life,* CA: Amber Allen Publishing & New World. Library

Richard Carlson, Ph.D. (2001). *Don't Sweat the Small Stuff About Money,* NY: Hyperion

Audio Programs

Chopra M.D., Deepak. *The Higher Self – The Magic of Inner and Outer Fulfillment,* IL: Nightingale-Conant.

Kiyosaki, Robert T. *Rich Dad Secrets To Money, Business and Investing... and How You can Profit from Them,* IL: Nightingale-Conant.

Magazines

O The Oprah Magazine, NY: Hearst Communications
New Age Magazine, MA: New Age Publishing
Open Minds Magazine, WI: Open Minds, Inc.

Websites

http://home.att.net/~quotations/death.html
http://home.att.net/~wbaustin/death.html
http://www.annabelle.net/topics/death.html
http://www.choosetobehappy.com/quotes.html
http://www.spiritsong.com/quotes/#quotes
http://www.theportableschool.com/BabyDoctor/Reincarnation.hml
http://www.healpastlives.com/pastlf/quote/qureincr.htm
http://www.geocities.com/joellescott/Biography.html
  (Scott Hamilton)
http://www.lkwdpl.org/wihohio/rudo-wil.htm
http://www.gale.com/freresrc/blkhstry/rudolph.htm
http://www.kron.com/specials/blackhistory/rudolph.html
http://www.cybernation.com/victory/quotations/subjects/quotes_
  negativity.html
http://www.zeta.org.au/~nps/cynicism/quotes/en/
http://www.gosalesgo.com/quotes/archive/mgandhi.html
http://www.motivationalquotes.com
http://butterflywebsite.com/articles/sendmon.htm
http://pprsites.tripod.com/pprquotes/PPR-Quotes-Idleness.htm
http://www.geocities.com/pprquotes/PPR-Quotes-Happiness.htm
http://www.worldwildlife.org/travel/listings/monarchs02.htm.

You Better Recognize!

Journal
for your-Self

Letters of Forgiveness

Dear Richard,

It's 3:00 in the morning and I can't sleep. I haven't been able to sleep for more than two hours at a time since you senselessly raped and murdered my wife. You took everything away from me when you killed her, Richard. Everything. I can not begin to describe the despair and grief... the emptiness that I feel since you took her away from me.

I am writing this letter to you because the author of a book that I came across suggested that if I tell you how I feel it might be help me to work through and let go of the anger and hatred I feel toward you. Maybe if I do, I can open myself up to the possibility of moving on with my life. I don't know if it will work, but I suppose anything is possible and I can't sleep anyway, so I'm going to try it.

There have been many nights that I lay here for hours, Richard... for hours trying to figure out why. Why did you have to kill her? Why? You of all people should know what a kind, giving spirit she was. The only thing that she ever did to you is to try to help you.

Do you have any idea what it is like to be totally in love with another human being? I bet you don't. Well, let me tell you. It's the most extraordinary feeling in the world. Now that's gone. Ros was the best thing that ever happened to me. She was the love and the light of my life. We were supposed to grow old together and take our grandchildren to the zoo and to the park. Now we can never do that. I'm angry at you for taking her and that away from me. I'm angry at her for leaving me. I'm angry at you for taking your own life. I didn't want you to die. You don't deserve death, because now you are at peace. And I'm still here. I don't want to be here, Richard. Not without Ros.

She must have been so scared. My heart is pained every time I think about how afraid she must have been. Then I become enraged. Enraged at you, Richard. And then there's nothing I can do with it. There's nowhere I can go with it. Because you're six feet under, Richard. Six feet under.

I am desperately sad. I feel so desperately sad sometimes that I can hardly breathe. Most days, I don't even want to get out of bed. I just want to crawl back into the darkness because sleep is my only reprieve from the nightmare that you left me with. The nightmare that is now my life.

The book that I read says that I should recognize your humanity, Richard. No matter how despicable you may be, I should recognize your humanity. I guess you are human, aren't you Richard... or weren't you? But what kind of human being would want to cause so much pain in other peoples' lives, Richard? What were you thinking when you killed her, Richard? What? Maybe if I try hard to see you as a fellow human being, maybe I can understand why you did it, Richard. And maybe if I understand why you did it, maybe I can get past this.

I'm not exactly sure how this letter is supposed to help me, but I guess I will see how I feel tomorrow and the next day after that.

Good night, Richard.

Ellis

(This is a fictional example written by Valerie Rose)

Dear Curtis,

All I ever wanted to do was love you. That's all. That's a good thing, right? That's supposed to be a good thing. I don't understand what I did to deserve this. I trusted you. Now I feel betrayed. Marriage is supposed to be about love, commitment and trust. When you left me, I felt so hurt inside. You have no idea. And I'm still hurt. I feel like I've wasted all of these years being married to a person that I don't even know. I'm hurt. I'm angry and I am disappointed. I don't know if I can ever trust again. I'm afraid to trust again. I'm afraid to love again. But after reading this book that Karen gave me, I now realize that if I don't trust again, I am punishing myself. Because I am denying myself the possibility of happiness in the future. I understand now that by not forgiving you and letting it go, I am reliving the pain of your leaving me over and over and over again. If I am going to survive this thing, I have to focus my energies on me. Instead of focusing on you, I have to utilize my energy to create something new... something positive... something loving. I realize now that to forgive you is to set myself free to do that... create something new... something positive... something loving. I have to be free if I am going to be happy. I might get hurt again, but I've decided that love is worth the risk.

So, I forgive you Curtis and I wish you well.

Rachel

(This is a fictional example written by Valerie Rose)

Letters of Forgiveness

_____

_____

_____

_____

_____

_____

_____

_____

_____

_____

_____

_____

_____

_____

_____

_____

_____

_____

_____

_____

_____

_____

_____

_____

_____

Journal for your-Self

Affirmations

1. *I am going to do what I said I was going to do.*
2. *I love my good health.*
3. *I have an incredible sex life.*
4.
5.
6.
7.
8.
9.
10.
11.
12.
13.
14.
15.
16.
17.
18.
19.
20.

Design for Your Life

What if you could take out a pen and paper and design your life, not the way it is today, but the way you would like it to be? What would you write? What if after you answered this question, the world would around you said, "Okay," and responded accordingly. What would you write?

_____

_____

_____

_____

_____

_____

_____

_____

_____

_____

_____

_____

_____

_____

_____

_____

_____

_____

_____

_____

_____

Journal for your-Self

Creative Thoughts

_____

_____

_____

_____

_____

_____

_____

_____

_____

_____

_____

_____

_____

_____

_____

_____

_____

_____

_____

_____

_____

_____

_____

_____

_____

_____

_____

_____

_____

_____

_____

_____

_____

_____

_____

_____

_____

_____

_____

_____

_____

_____

_____

_____

_____

_____

_____

_____

Roses Are READ Productions
P. O. Box 7844
St. Paul, MN 55107
E-mail: valerie.rose @gte.net
Websites:
http://www.rosesareread.cc
http://www.valerierose.com

For additional copies of this book, do one
of the following:

- Visit your local book store.
- Call Midwest Book Distributors
  at 1-877-430-0044.
- Visit us online.

What people are saying about other books by Valerie Rose :

Cappuccino in the Winter

"A riveting, tender, and emotionally moving story. Valerie Rose has a remarkable talent for creating captivating characters. This beautiful story will live in the heart forever."
– Jacquelin Thomas, author of BET Books', *Hidden Blessings*

"Valerie's excellent choice in words quickly eat up the page, making one avarice to move on to partake of the next delicious course." – Linda Hudson-Smith, author of BET Books', *Ice Under Fire*

"...The reader enters the cyber world of computers; the plot is littered with intrigue. This novel would set a movie screen ablaze with action, romance and drama." – *Rendezvous Magazine*
"*Cappuccino in the Winter* steams with unquenchable passion and subterfuge. Take a sip and I promise you won't be able to put it down until the very last drop. – Rick Malone, author of *Violet of a Deeper Blue*

"An exciting tale of corporate politics, romance, and a bit of political intrigue. Here is a book that will call for your undivided attention as the book begins with a bang and only picks up its pace from there! I find myself looking forward to the next story—by Valerie Rose!" – HUNTRESS BOOK REVIEWS (Reviewed by Détra Fitch)

"...*CAPPUCCINO IN THE WINTER* will delight both computer aficionados and romance fans." – www.romanceincolor.com

The Family Reunion Is Not A Real Vacation

"A WONDERFUL BOOK... INSIGHTFUL... A book for all ages, espousing the virtues and fun of the time honoredfamily reunion." – Ken Burkeen, Book Channel Manager, BlackVoices.com

"An entertaining way of teaching children to value family." – F.M. Avey, author *The Harlequin's Nutcracker, Girl Gifts*

"In just a few short pages, *The Family Reunion Is Not A Real Vacation* took me down memory lane to my own family reunion as a child and as an adult. Valerie Rose connected the dots in showing children how family reunions truly can be a real vacation." – Sandra King Freeman, *Soulful Crosswords*

"I think this is a good book for kids to read. It teaches us that it is important and fun to spend time with our family." – Marlon Watts, Children's Book Reviewer, The Hook Up Network (TheHUNetwork) Empowerment Zone (e-Zone) Newsletter

About the Author

Valerie Rose, is a native of Milwaukee, Wisconsin, but has lived and worked in the Twin Cities for more than fifteen years. Her debut novel, *Cappuccino in the Winter* - a romantic suspense is set in the Twin Cities, was chosen by Michigan new comer, Avid Press, to launch their new Kismet imprint. A recommended new title in *Black Issues Book Review,* Cappuccino, although released in December 1999, is still doing well, selling out at the 2001 Romance Slam Jam held in Orlando, Florida.

Valerie, is the owner of Roses Are READ Productions, which has produced a range of literary work that has appeared in many local and national venues. Some of her writing credits include publications in: The View (from the Loft), Futures Magazine, Jive Magazine, The Black Data Processing Journal, The St. Paul Recorder and The Minneapolis Spokesman.

A featured author at the 2001 Congressional Black Caucus Foundation's Annual Legislative Conference, Valerie Rose draws attention from both the local and national media. Her many appearances and interviews run the gamut, including among others: Milwaukee Public Television's Black Nouveau (news magazine program), Write On! Radio, The Freddie Bell Morning Show, nationally syndicated ABC Radio Network, Twin Cities Women of Color Expo: The Gathering, The Jamaican Observer Tourist Times, and Shades of Romance, an online magazine.

Valerie is a member of the Loft Literary Center, The Romance Writers of America and the Midwest Fiction Writers. She lives in Minneapolis with her two children, where she is busy at work on her next project.